ANIMALS IN DANGER

CHRISTIAN ZUBER

ANIMALS IN DANGER

Translated from the French
by J.F. Bernard

BARRONS/WOODBURY, NEW YORK

First U.S. edition 1978 by Barron's Educational Series, Inc.

L'Arche de Noé

© Flammarion, 1974

© Galapagos Films

All inquiries should be addressed to:
Barron's Educational Series, Inc.
113 Crossways Park Drive
Woodbury, New York 11797

Library of Congress Catalog Card No. 78–57593

International Standard Book No. 0–8120–5281–1

Library of Congress Cataloging in Publication Data

Zuber, Christian, 1930-
  Animals in danger.

  Translation of L'Arche de Noé.
  Bibliography: p.
  Includes index.
  1. Rare animals. I. Title
QL82.Z8213   596   78-57593
ISBN 0-8120-5281-1

PRINTED IN HONG KONG

TABLE OF CONTENTS

Corbett Park, in the north of India, is one of the few remaining places in the world where one can see tigers roaming at large in the jungle.

Princes of the jungle

The last great adventure

The roar was like a clap of thunder, deafening, cavernous, interminable. Fear tore the camera from my eye, and my guide stumbled against me as he retreated in terror. Once before, in an automobile accident, I had had this feeling: there was nothing to do but wait. It was all over, and we must prepare ourselves for the worst. The jungle itself had been shocked into silence by that giant roar. Stooping as much as I could, I gathered the camera and tripod in my arms before beginning a slow, stealthy retreat toward the Landrover. My wife edged forward, accompanied by two Indians who were green with fear. "Christian," she whispered. "Be careful. He's coming!"

Between us and the tiger, about a hundred yards away, was the half-devoured carcass of a water buffalo killed the night before. Despite his anger at having been disturbed by us, the tiger paused and fixed his yellow eyes upon us. There was a moment of absolute immobility—then he threw himself on the carcass and, with much crashing and splintering of branches, dragged it into the underbrush. Once more, our luck had held. The Landrover had been left behind on the path; and, as usual, our only weapons were our cameras.

I looked at the gauge on the camera: three minutes of film. In seven weeks, we had shot three minutes of film! The explanation was simple: there are virtually no tigers left in India. As we shall see, these splendid carnivores are on the road to extinction.

A world without tigers! And not only tigers. Other mammals, birds, reptiles, plants, crustaceans, thousands of fishes—all are equally threatened.

The problem has received much publicity, but comparatively few people know the facts on the currently very fashionable subject of environmental protection. In many cases, opinions are formed on the basis of statistics and reports that are seldom more than theoretical and

hypothetical. It is my job to try to search out the facts *in situ*. My vocation is to bring back documents, statistics, photographs, and tape recordings of what is now becoming the greatest slaughter of animals in the history of the world. My purpose is to exhibit my findings on television; for in this audiovisual era, I am convinced that television is the most effective of all the means of communication. If nature is to be saved, then it is television that will save it—although that statement will not please everyone who reads it.

The sequence on tigers in India was our last great adventure before we began working with the "super monkeys"; that is, gorillas, chimpanzees, and orangutans. It was an adventure that had begun ten years earlier entirely by chance, as in a romantic novel, as the result of an unexpected encounter.

The other person in the encounter was Sir Peter Scott, the son of Robert Scott, the twentieth-century explorer of Antarctica and an environmentalist, writer, painter, champion seaman, ornithologist, world-renowned specialist in anatidae (an aquatic family of birds, including ducks, swans, geese), and a man wealthy in the riches that come to those who know how to listen, to narrate, and to travel.

When I first met Sir Peter Scott, looked into his quizzical eyes and saw his smiling face, I had not the slightest suspicion that our meeting would change my life.

With Sir Peter Scott

We met on the Galápagos Islands in the Pacific Ocean. I had left France alone, three months before, with my luggage strapped to my back and my camera slung over my shoulder, to film "the strangest land in the world." In fact, however, I was fascinated by the somewhat exceptional life-style of the Europeans living on the islands, and I lived hippie-style without doing much more than going out with the fishermen as they worked the waters of that prehistoric archipelago. The familiarity with the area that I gained stood me in good stead. I was asked by Jean Dorst, who was then assistant curator of the Museum of Natural History in Paris, to give whatever help I could to a British Broadcasting Corporation expedition to the islands. The head of that expedition, as it happened, was Sir Peter Scott.

I therefore offered my amateur services to that television professional and to his wife, Phil—a joyous photographer and a brilliant cook—and to the expedition's cameraman, Tony Sopher, a delightful Englishman.

After a day spent filming the spectacular courting of the frigate birds of Tower Island (Genovesa), Peter spoke to me for the first time of the World Wildlife Fund, an organization of which he was secretary-general. I learned that the W.W.F. had as its chief sponsor Prince Bernhard of the Netherlands, and that its headquarters staff was stationed in Morges, Switzerland. It is a nonpolitical organization and an effective one; one that carries great moral weight. Over a dozen nations were cooperating in its environmental protection program.

What particularly interested me about the W.W.F. was its financial aspect; that is, the organization's position with regard to money. For it would be very naive to think that any project, no matter how worthy, can get off the ground without ample funds. We have only to look at the record—at the thousands of societies, groups, and associations that, despite their good intentions and their determination to "do something," have failed and vanished in the recent past. Good intentions do not suffice, even if they are accompanied by an outstretched palm.

It is an accepted fact of modern life that money destroys, money pollutes, money kills. But money can also protect, preserve, and save. The problem is to find the money to do the latter. And that is where the W.W.F. comes in.

Rome was not built in a day, and neither was the W.W.F. The organization very wisely took the time to solidify its structure before initiating its financial campaign. A very simple basic formula was adopted: one-third of each contribution is used in the donating country; the remaining two-thirds is used for purposes of environmental protection in other nations. Not one cent goes to "administrative expenses" or "management fees" or any similar use. The staff and headquarters in Switzerland cost nothing so far as the countries affiliated with the W.W.F. are concerned. Also, there is no cumbersome machinery involved in the approval of expenditures by the Fund, and monies are made immediately available. Nature does not wait for the decisions of an Executive Committee. In environmental protection, there is no such thing as a non-urgent matter.

So much for the Fund's financial situation. These finances are used solely for conservation projects of various kinds adapted to circumstances, to the country, to the species involved, and also to the possibilities of protection. There is a standing list of urgent cases that is kept current on a daily basis through the efforts of on-the-spot correspondents and of various study groups.

There are about twenty people at the headquarters office at Morges who work full time—and sometimes more than full time—for the Fund. How can a secretary not be enthusiastic about his or her work when the

Opposite: The jet may well be the means of transportation most used by explorers today, although other forms of transportation seem to allow us "more time for living." One example: riding an elephant at Kasiranga, behind the mahout who pilots the animal.

current project is "A Report on the Preservation of the Northern Square-Lipped Rhinoceros"? Or a department head when he can pick up a telephone and announce, "We're sending you two radios to use against the poachers"? Or the members of a group who are having a cup of tea to celebrate the arrival of an unexpected check earmarked "for the protection of the Scimitar-horned oryx"?

Like any association, the headquarters has specialized sections. It also has representatives from all member countries. There are two annual meetings, both planned far in advance, which bring together conservationists from the four corners of the earth. Finally, an important detail: all committee members are unpaid volunteers.

All the work at headquarters, in the field, and at the international conferences proceeds according to a very well-defined program. The ideal is to waste no time or money, to undertake no useless project. Effectiveness is given the highest priority.

So far as I was concerned, I made a decision: I would devote part of my time to the pleasure of working for the World Wildlife Fund. And, believe me, it is a very rare pleasure indeed. That which is not paid for is often the most difficult thing to acquire. To me, one form of happiness is being able to say: "My job is my avocation."

Modern life

I was in Paris, working on the layout of a children's book, when the telephone rang. A call from Morges, Switzerland. I knew that the W.W.F. did not make telephone calls simply to pass the time of day.

"Hello? Christian Zuber? It's Fritz Wollmar. Listen, we're starting a big operation aimed at protecting tigers. We're going to need some film and some photographs."

"I see," I replied somewhat lamely. "When do you need them?"

"As soon as possible! We already need the film and some copies and about fifty photographs!"

Fritz Wollmar, director general of the Fund, is a man of action rather than of words. He did not give me a second in which to think about the problems involved, but hurried on: "I've already notified our correspondents in New Delhi. They're going to handle everything on that end. All you have to do is get ready and get over there. I'm sending you everything we have on tigers. And don't forget to bring a suit for the receptions. Madam Gandhi is behind us on this. That's about it. *Bon voyage.* And don't forget to put a tiger in your camera!"

Fritz hung up, leaving me with the receiver still in my hand. I sat momentarily stunned as visions of Kipling danced in my head.

Theoretically, I'm always ready at a moment's notice to hop into the first available airplane and to go film or photograph anything anywhere in the world. So far as preparation is concerned, a simple job of reporting is translated into six small aluminum suitcases. More complicated jobs—underwater shots or filming wild animals—require more complex equipment: twelve suitcases. There is no difficulty with film, since I always have some on hand. In other words, if it were merely a matter of equipment. I could leave almost as soon as I was notified of an assignment.

What makes it impossible for me, or anyone else, simply to jump on a plane are the obstacles created by civilization: visas, permits, customs, lists of matériel, authorizations, forms, photographs, signatures, stamps, and other such brilliant inventions. Even with official support, personal contacts, the smiles of secretaries, and the good will of customs officials, we waste an incredible amount of time wandering through our labyrinthine bureaucracies. It is my firm conviction that, unless you are willing to lie, cheat, forge, and falsify (which, I confess, I am not above doing), you could spend a month trying to leave one country and enter another.

One of the most irritating things for a traveler to a so-called developing country—i.e., a country that was once the colony of a "developed country"—is the fact that the new country invariably has retained its Western-style bureaucracy and its addiction to paperwork. Occasionally, however, one finds a representative of such a country who has not sold his or her soul for a filing cabinet. I have in mind a very charming secretary at one of the African embassies in Paris—a truly beautiful woman who, fortunately, did not choose to dress in European clothes. She welcomed me with a smile to the visa bureau. "All right," she said, "I'll need your passport and two photographs."

I handed her the passport and photographs. "Oh," she said, laughing, "you're not very good-looking in these pictures. You're better in real life! Never mind. Now, take these four forms and fill them out. You can use that desk over there."

She handed me four blue sheets of paper. I spread them on the desk she had indicated and began to fill them out, feeling as though I had been kept after school. When I finished, I handed them to her. She read them carefully. Suddenly she looked up. "Sir, you've made a mistake here, where you're supposed to fill in your address. First, your home address, and then the address of your place of employment. You've put the same address for both. That's obviously incorrect."

"But I work at home."

"You don't understand. Here, on this line, is the address of your home, your house, where you sleep. Is that right?"

"Right."

"And here, on this next line, is supposed to be the address of the

place where you work. Your office. It's not the same thing. You can't have the same address for both!"

"But my home and my office are both the same!"

The woman's smile vanished and she thrust the blue forms at me, pointing to them with a long, brown finger. Because she was so lovely, I managed to keep my temper in check.

"Obviously, sir, I'm going to have to go over the whole thing with you once more." She began explaining, slowly, patiently, as she had learned to do in a European school. I said not a word. Then, finally, her common sense prevailed over her training. "Wait a minute," she said. "I see that I already have your visa here, all signed and stamped. These forms—well, now we don't need these forms at all." And, with that, she thrust the sheets of paper into a drawer and slammed it shut. For all I know, the four blue forms are still in that drawer.

The last tigers?

"What the hell do I care if there aren't any more tigers? I don't give a damn about your campaign!"

These words were spoken, in great anger, by an apparently average Frenchman, when we approached him on the street. He then crumpled the handbill that we had given him and, taking his wife by the arm, disappeared into the crowd. It was the third time that, along with a half-dozen enthusiastic young supporters, we had distributed our handbills along the Champs-Elysées in Paris. We did not give them to just anyone. We waited until we spotted someone, man or woman, wearing a coat, jacket, or collar made from the skins of one of the endangered species of spotted cats. Then, very politely, we handed them an envelope containing a half-page of information on the fur-bearing species in danger of extinction. Our approach to such people was governed by very strict ground rules: always smile; never accept even the smallest contribution; pick up the envelope if the recipient throws it on the ground. And, finally, disappear at the first sight of a policeman because it is against French law to distribute handbills on a public street—which did not prevent me from filming everything without the slightest hindrance from the cops.

The handbill itself was quite clear and to the point. The following words were printed on the envelope: "Madame, this is not an advertisement but a message which concerns you personally."

Opposite: Wild animals born in captivity—and tigers particularly—cannot be turned loose again in the jungle. They do not know how to defend themselves or to flee from man or, above all, how to hunt for food. The breeding of animals in zoos (here, at Kuala Lumpur in Malaysia) allows captive animals to be exchanged, but it does not serve to replenish the supply of free animals.

Above: The white tiger is an albino. Because they are so rare, white tigers are an attraction for zoos.

Below: The South American jaguar is the New World equivalent of the African leopard or panther.

The fur of this young serval, who lives in the Ethiopian bush, is highly prized by furriers. Below is the Chinese leopard. A pair of these animals lives in the Colombo Zoo in Sri Lanka (formerly Ceylon).

Inside the envelope was an equally polite note printed on W.W.F. stationery:

Madame,

You are wearing a garment made from the skin of a spotted cat.

It's likely that you've had the coat for a while, and that you bought it before it was known that these animals are in danger of becoming extinct.

Today, however, this is general knowledge. Everyone has learned that if the slaughter of these animals is not stopped, tigers, jaguars, panthers, leopards, and ocelots will disappear from the face of the earth within a few years.

The spotted cats are a legacy from the past; a part of our human heritage, just as historical monuments are part of that heritage—and perhaps more, for a monument created by man can be replaced by man, while there is no power on earth that can recreate an extinct species.

It is therefore absolutely necessary to put a halt to the slaughter of these animals, to the selling of their furs, and to the wearing of these furs. This has been demonstrated by the International Union for the Conservation of Nature and Natural Resources (IUCN) and by the World Wildlife Fund, which have brought the situation to the attention of various national governments. Several countries have already outlawed the importation of the fur of spotted cats, and the International Federation of Furriers has recommended that its members withdraw these furs from the market.

We do not suggest that you destroy your garment or otherwise dispose of it, since this will make no difference with respect to the already endangered species. What we do ask is that you refrain from wearing this garment so as to discourage other women from wearing theirs.

When there is no more consumer demand for these furs, the furriers will no longer market them. At that point, trade in these skins will come to a halt, and there will be no reason to hunt and kill these animals.

If you comply with this request, you will be contributing to the salvation of these animals; and, in saving them, you will be preserving one of the glories of nature for future generations.

If you wear this fur in London or in New York, you risk being unpleasantly conspicuous because the message you have received is known to the general public of these cities.

If you accept our suggestion, we would be grateful for a letter to that effect.

World Wildlife Fund
Morges, Switzerland

The wildcat of Sri Lanka has been hunted so freely that it is almost extinct. The above specimen was photographed at the Colombo Zoo. Below is the Iranian cheetah, distinguished from the African cheetah by its longer, thicker tail. It no longer exists in the wild, and this male is probably the last living member of his species.

TIGERS OF THE WORLD		
Species	Estimated Number	Status
Bali tiger	0	Extinct
Siberian tiger	60 to 70	Extinction likely
Chinese tiger	fewer than 50	Extinction likely
Indochinese tiger	over large area, fewer than 2,000	Extinction likely in less than 20 years
Sumatran tiger	fewer than 100	Extinction likely
Javan tiger	5	Extinction certain
Caspian tiger	15	Extinction certain
Indian tiger	less than 2,000	May be saved

These three cats are all in danger of becoming extinct: the cheetah, the European lynx, and the African leopard. Furriers in Europe, America, and Japan are responsible for their extinction. Their intensive advertising campaigns, coupled with the offers to buy skins from poachers, have resulted in the near disappearance of these species.

The letter is not a demand, but an effort at transmitting information. Here are a few statistics concerning the reactions of people who were handed the letter. Of the women approached, 58% said that they had bought their furs before they knew anything about endangered species; 21% still knew nothing about the issue; and the remaining 21% could not have cared less one way or the other. On the other hand, 80% of the people approached in Paris accepted the handbill—although 5% of those who accepted it threw it away a few seconds later. The rest of them registered a reaction identical to that described above: indignation, anger.

Sixty years ago, before the terms *conservation, ecology,* and *pollution* became part of the public vocabulary, it was noted that there had been a severe reduction in the number of tigers in India. A group of scientists, in collaboration with the Forestry Office and the Hunting Office, decided to take a census of the animals. The census method was based on three principles: first, that tigers drink at least three times a week; second, that every tiger or tiger family has a well-defined territory; and, finally, that every tiger has a distinctive foot-print. Finally, after painstaking preparations, the census began. Bait, in the form of car-

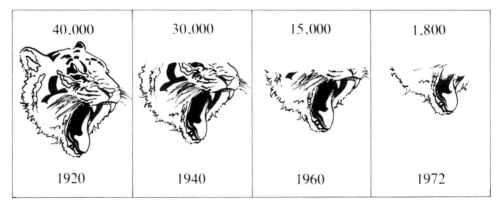

40,000	30,000	15,000	1,800
1920	1940	1960	1972

casses of animals, was set out at hundreds of marked locations in the jungle. The areas around the water holes and the carcasses were then covered with a layer of ashes so as to have a record of the tigers' footprints. On the given day, simultaneously throughout the whole of India, tracings were made of all the footprints in the ashes.

At that point, the census actually began. First, the prints of other animals—even pythons—were identified and discarded. Then, in order to reduce the chance of counting the same animal twice (the territories of old tigers sometimes include or overlap those of young tigers) the total number of identifiable tigers was reduced by 15%. After painstaking calculations and verifications—all this, of course, was before the age of calculators and computers—it was determined that there were approximately 42,000 tigers in India at that time. That sounds like a large number of tigers. However, we must bear in mind that the tiger is a predator; that is, an animal that maintains the ecological balance of nature by preying on a certain number of animals of other species. Thus, in relation to the very large herds of deer, all of which are the tiger's natural prey, a population of 42,000 tigers is not large at all, particularly when one remembers that the Indian subcontinent at that time covered an area equal to almost half the territory of the United States.

In 1972, another census was made, using the same methods in the same places, and conducted by a similar group of British and Indian researchers, forestry experts, guards, and conservationists. The results were alarming. There were only 1800 tigers alive in India. From 42,000 to less than 2,000 in fifty-two years!

These statistics in themselves justify the urgent nature of the information-gathering process on tigers, the in-depth study of the reasons for the near-extinction of these animals, and the organization of a program for the protection of the surviving animals. It also justifies our seven-week expedition to India, our two television films, our 700 photographs—and the chapter that you are now reading.

Spotted furs

The rapid disappearance of the species of spotted felines is the result of a chain of events that is extremely difficult to break. The first link in this chain is the consumer, the man or woman who wants to be fashionable, to satisfy his or her vanity, or occasionally even to gratify a taste for beautiful things. The second link, which is the strongest and the most dangerous to nature, is the furrier. The furrier is the individual ultimately responsible for the tragedy. It is the furrier who buys and sells. He operates at two levels and makes a profit at both levels. He encourages the hunter to kill and the consumer to buy. After the furrier comes a series of middlemen, distributors, traders, etc., down to the men who do the actual hunting. The hunters themselves are most often poor, ignorant men who are totally unaware of the value of the skins that they hunt—skins which, at the other end of the chain, sell for enormous sums, as we shall see with respect to tiger skins.

We should keep in mind that it is the furrier who is at the helm and is responsible for this slaughter of animals. The furrier controls the market by stocking skins and maintaining a brisk traffic in them; thus he is able to sell furs at a very high price even when there is an abundant supply of them. We've made film of enormous stockpiles of furs in Switzerland. The owners of those skins admitted unblushingly that they buy them and put them aside. When prices go up, they sell them, a few at a time. Fur traders in the jungle do the same thing. Despite the danger in-

We baited this leopard in Sri Lanka with a piece of meat so that we could photograph it. Sri Lanka is one of the few places in the world where we can still see wild leopards even during the daylight hours, and especially at water holes.

volved—there is always the possibility of a raid by the police—traders who buy directly from poachers always have a stock of old skins on the premises. When a poacher arrives with a skin, the trader shows him his stock even before talking price. In other words, he shows the poacher that he doesn't need the skin, and that it isn't worth much to him. In 1973, in a shop in Singapore, I saw a Malaysian sell five panther skins (one of which had been taken from an animal of no more than six months), for a mouthful of bread. I'll never forget the smirk on the face of the trader when, after the seller had left the shop, I picked up one of the skins in his "stock." It was so old that the fur came off in my hand.

The same little commercial drama is played out in East Africa. An Indian trader watches two Masai hunters enter his shop carrying some magnificent serval skins. The skins are fresh, still dripping blood. No words are exchanged. The trader leads the hunters into the back room and raises the lid of a large box. The box is filled with leopard skins neatly folded and stacked. The lid is lowered and the Masai have understood. For their serval skins, they will get a few pieces of paper money and not one cent more. Before they leave, the shopkeeper adds a word of warning: he is acquainted with several policemen who are looking for poachers. The Masai understand that, too. It means that if they try to sell their skins elsewhere, they will be in trouble with the police.

This kind of exploitation is as continuous as it is deplorable. It often happens that the authorities do, in fact, confiscate some skins and imprison a poacher. (The traders themselves seem never to be arrested.) Then, after an interminable investigation and volumes of paperwork, the confiscated skins are locked in a warehouse. Shortly thereafter, they disappear mysteriously; no one seems to care since, at least on paper, the requirements of the law have been satisfied.

I should point out again that I am talking only about the skins of spotted felines. I am not calling for a ban on all traffic in furs. I am the happy owner of a sheepskin coat. It is warm, comfortable, and indispensable on expeditions. There are a sufficient number of other species to allow people to cover themselves with the skins of animals if they wish to do so—species that are not in any danger of extinction. For our purposes, therefore, we may divide fur-bearing animals into those which may be exploited commercially, those which must be protected and preserved, and those which fall somewhere between the first and second groups. Here, generally, without worrying about scientific groupings, is a breakdown of those three categories:

First category: Fur-bearing animals bred in captivity by man, such as mink, chinchilla, rabbits, sheep, sable, etc. These furs may be worn.

Second category: Fur-bearing wild animals in imminent danger of extinction because they have been overexploited. A complete list would take an entire page; so, I will mention only the better known of the spotted cats: tigers, panthers, jaguars, snow leopards, cheetahs, lynx, and ocelot. (To that, let us add a few nonfelines: seals, giant pandas, white bears, grizzly bears, otters, and vicunas.) No one should ever buy, or wear, the furs of these animals.

Third category: Fur-bearing wild animals hunted for their skins which are still plentiful—foxes (but not all species), beavers (in certain countries)—but the skins of which one should avoid wearing so as not to endanger the species.

Every year, new names are added to the list of endangered species, and these are only the known species. There are, no doubt, species which become extinct without ever coming to the attention of the public.

Many misinformed people, when they hear of animals on the verge of extinction, say, "It's perfectly natural. After all, the dinosaurs are extinct!" In speaking of endangered species in the twentieth century, we are not speaking of the natural process of extinction by virtue of which dinosaurs disappeared from the earth. We are talking about species that are disappearing because of human beings—species exterminated not by nature, but by slaughter and by the conditions of life in the twentieth century.

Documents and images

In our quest for documentation on spotted felines, we made five expeditions to Africa, one to Ceylon, and two to India. In our opinion, we must have some knowledge of the life and behavior, as well as of the number, of animals belonging to the endangered species if we are to know how to protect those species. This is an undertaking requiring much time and labor. Any error at the scientific level may result in a real catastrophe. Some of these studies are rather delicate, and the process of observation of certain phenomena (migrations, nocturnal life, habits of marine animals, habits of species inhabiting dangerous or inaccessible areas) is extremely complex—as we discovered at Tromelin Island in the Indian Ocean, when we tried to observe sea turtles in the breakers and surf around the island.

It is particularly difficult to film panthers in Africa, even though the task is somewhat facilitated by the fact that panthers tend to move around a great deal at night. It is possible to get one or two close-ups of an animal walking along a jungle path on his way to a waterhole or sleeping in an acacia tree. But two close-ups don't make a film.

It is worth noting here that a famous sequence, which appeared in *Life* magazine several years ago, showing a panther attacking and killing

Above: Christian Zuber, "Tiger Man," and Brij Singh during the 1972 expedition. The baby tiger in the photo on the left is a semi-albino—hence his light fur. Two specimens were born at the New Delhi Zoo, one of the most beautiful zoological gardens in the world.
Opposite: Poachers in Assam have set fire to the bush. In these areas, the destruction of the environment by fire is one of the most serious problems of parks and wild animal preserves.

a baboon, was an entirely staged affair. A trained panther was turned loose within an enclosure, along with a number of wild monkeys. According to an eyewitness, "It was a real massacre. Four monkeys were killed before we could get a picture." The same magazine financed another project: the photographing of gazelles being killed by a (trained) cheetah. Despite the best efforts of the organizers of the scheme, and of the dozen or so terrified gazelles, the cheetah did not manage to make a single kill. What everybody seemed to have forgotten was that a cat raised by humans is handicapped for life and cannot return to the wild. His instincts are atrophied; his speed is inadequate; he is soon out of breath. And, above all, the animal does not know the techniques of hunting, bringing down, and killing his prey. He had no mother to teach him to feed himself; his muscles, nerves, claws, and fangs were never trained for survival.

A large number of conservationists have spoken out against the misguided attitude adopted by certain curators of zoos who try to "protect nature" and "preserve species" by breeding animals in captivity, creating shelters for rare animals, and even by turning loose animals born in captivity so as to "give them back their freedom."

There have been rare instances in which this method has worked: the Scimitar-horned oryx of Arabia, the Nene goose of Hawaii, and a few other cases which one can count on the fingers of one hand. But it

simply does not work for the vast majority of wild animals, and it works not at all for feline species. All efforts in that direction have ended in failure. And, although much publicity is given to the initial attempt, no publicity at all accompanies the failures that follow.

One interesting case occurred not long ago, when a half dozen lion cubs were sent from Paris to Africa so as "to be set free in the country of their origin." The cubs were turned loose in a game preserve and, for the first few months, everything seemed to go well. The cubs, no doubt delighted to be able to romp in the African sun, grew rapidly. Soon they were on a steady diet of meat. Gradually, they edged into the jungle, following the tracks of living prey and forgetting entirely the bars and fences of their youth. There was only one problem: not a single one of the lions was ever able to make a kill on his own. And it was not for lack of opportunity. Captured gazelles were turned loose before the lions, practically under their noses, and they shot across the savannahs like arrows, too fast for the lions to catch. Finally, a live donkey was offered to the now famished cats, and the slaughter that resulted shocked and disgusted a group of passing tourists, who decried the incident. Finally, there seemed to be nothing to do but to treat the lions as though they were still in captivity; that is, to give them a ration of meat every evening.

The price of meat in Africa is just as high as in Europe or America, and the feeding of the lions created a financial situation which, apparently, could not be endured. A few weeks later, rifle shots were heard at the edge of the jungle, and the chief guard's Landrover was seen making its way slowly back to camp. The history of the lions "set free" in Africa was over.

The zoos

We should note that, although it is rare that man can preserve the world's "natural capital" by raising animals in cages, the "captive natural capital"—i.e., the species that are able to reproduce in decent captivity—represent a positive element in the conservation of species. Certainly, it is better to have certain animals reproduce in captivity than to have them disappear altogether from the face of the earth—the tiger, for instance, as well as the bison, the brown bear, the python, the okapi, and many other rare animals. Dr. Lang, director of the Basel Zoo—one of Europe's best—has been successful in starting a family of single-horned rhinoceroses which, along with the zoo's large monkeys, are the great attraction of the institution. In Germany, Dr. Grzimek, director of the Frankfurt Zoo, has been successful in reproducing many rare species in captivity, including a family of gorillas which inhabits, not a cage, but a large, shaded open space. Needless to say, the gorillas are a unique spectacle which attracts thousands of visitors.

These are examples to be followed and encouraged with as much enthusiasm as we use in deploring and condemning the sad spectacle of animal exploitation in captivity.

Eight "species" of tiger*

Jungle movies have popularized the image of the Bengal tiger. And, since Kipling's *Jungle Book*, the figure of Sheerkhan has haunted the dreams of anyone who has longed to voyage to India to see this prince of the jungle in his raiment of gold and black. But those who know tigers rarely use the term *Bengal tiger*, for the simple reason that this animal is found not only in Bengal, but also in other parts of the Indian subcontinent. It is noteworthy that there have never been tigers in Ceylon, while other cats, such as the panther, are plentiful on that island.

The Indian tiger is not the largest of its kind. An adult male measures from eight to nine and one-half feet in length (from the tip of his nose to the tip of his tail). A record of twelve feet, two inches was set in 1932 by an animal that had been shot and was measured before being cut up. (The importance of measuring before skinning is that the skin can be stretched; and, as with claims of snakes forty feet long, some mighty hunters have unblushingly claimed to have brought down tigers even longer than twelve feet, two inches.)

Even apart from his fur and markings, the appearance of a tiger seems to vary considerably from that of a lion. Yet, as one professional hunter has remarked, "If you put a skinned lion next to a skinned tiger, it's impossible to tell which is which."

And, speaking of lions, we should point out that lions and tigers can crossbreed. A number of such hybrids may be found in the private menagerie of the sultan of Morocco, Muhammed V. If the cub's father is a tiger, the cub is called a tigon; if he is a lion, the cub is a liger. Obviously, these animals are nothing more than curiosities in certain zoos whose owners have more interest in the unusual than they have respect for their animals. This kind of crossbreeding is noticeable in the intermixing of "species" among tigers presented for public viewing. The uncontrolled mating of these animals in captivity has led to an unbelievable

*Scientists classify tigers not by species, but by race and subspecies.

Double page following: Dev Goswami is one of those rare men who have been attacked by a tiger and lived to tell the story. His attacker was an enormous male, as shown by the wax mold of the tiger's print. Dev escaped with eight months in the hospital and a set of scars on his right thigh.

These leopards are the last born in captivity at Naivasha. The government of Kenya has forbidden private citizens to have wild animals in their homes, even though they may be tamed.

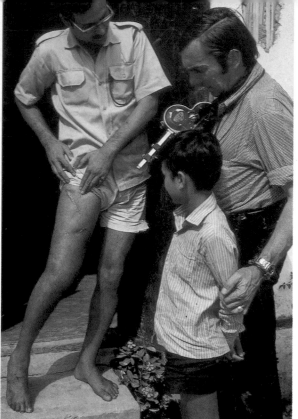

Corbett Park, in India, would be an ideal preserve for the last tigers—if only the country's Forestry Service could resist exploiting the jungle for lumber. This animal's hide is worth seven months' salary to a woodcutter.

confusion of subspecies—so much so that, as often as not, the sign identifying the occupant of a cage is misleading.

The variation in the color of tigers is considerable and ranges from brick red, through all shades of yellow, to beige. The tiger's stripes are often very dark, particularly on the head.

Our observation of tigers in the field and in captivity revealed a high degree of individuality in the stripes of tigers. Not only are these more or less pronounced markings different from one tiger to the next, but also the white spots around the eyes vary in design.

There have been comparative studies of the shape and size of the skulls of tigers, which reveal that some ''species'' have larger skulls

These photographs, taken in daylight by Nadine, at a distance of ninety feet, shows how calm these giant felines are when they are not being hunted. It also evidences their indifference to the presence of humans.

than others. There are also differences in fur, which is thicker in tigers inhabiting colder areas (Siberia, for example), and thinner, for instance, among the few surviving specimens of Sumatran tiger. In Sumatra, tigers often suffer from the heat and spend hours at a time in the water. For the tiger, unlike many other cats, loves to swim and will often take to a river or pool. In the heat of the Indian summer, we filmed one tiger who spent two hours lying in a stream north of Calcutta. There are many directors of zoos whose walls are covered with diplomas but who somehow have managed to remain ignorant of the tiger's taste for water.

A male tiger lives alone in his territory, except during the mating

season and during the period in which the female is raising her young. In optimum conditions, a litter comprises four or five cubs. Usually, two or three of the cubs reach maturity.

Getting started

A cameraman-explorer generally has two different approaches to his work. The first is to prepare for an expedition by long and arduous months of work, reading every book and article available on a particular subject, studying every photograph and every film that he can lay his hands on. He spends endless hours checking and double-checking his equipment and making certain that everything he could possibly need is on hand—and sometimes in duplicate. His thirteen or fifteen aluminum trunks are packed. All administrative papers, vaccination certificates, filming permits, letters of introduction and recommendation, customs lists and other such necessities of human civilization are carefully arranged in a briefcase of their own.

The second approach is very different. The telephone rings. Something important to the conservation movement is happening elsewhere in the world. A decision has to be made immediately, and you must be on the next plane. . . . For this kind of operation, we use a minimum of equipment—what I call, from my experience with the military, my "commando gear": some photographic and film equipment; a passport; a toothbrush.

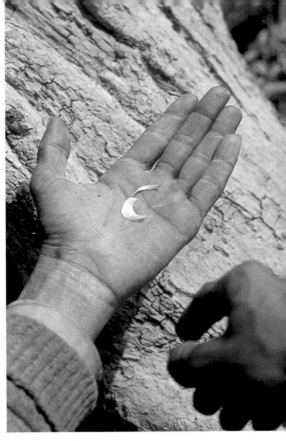

The axis deer (chital), which are the staple of tigers, have also lessened in number because of excessive hunting. Twice a week, a tiger comes to sharpen his claws (above) on this tree trunk. The animal's tracks (below), along with the evidence on the tree trunk, make it possible to determine a tiger's territory.

No preparation, regardless of how complete it may be, and no departure, no matter how hurried, can take the place of an essential element in any expedition: personal contact with people who live in the country that you are visiting. Except for my first job for *Paris-Match* in the Galapagos Islands, which I undertook alone, my voyages in the past ten years have always been as part of a team. On all those expeditions, we have always had help—and sometimes very important help, as far as results were concerned—from people whom we met in the field. Thus, in India, without the selfless and very effective aid of Robin Banerjee, Arjan Singh, Brijindra Singh, and above all Ann Wright, we would never have been able to bring back our two films on *The Princes of the Jungle.*

The story of a man and a tiger

Shortly before leaving for India, I had a telephone call from Hettier de Boislambert, the head of Compagnons de la Liberation,* who told me: "If you get permission to go into Assam, make sure you stop at Kasiranga. There's a magnificent preserve there, where you can look at the rhinoceroses from the back of an elephant. And, while you're there, mention my name and ask to see Dev Goswami, one of the guards. He can tell you everything you want to know about tigers."

We had every intention of following this advice. Before visiting Kasiranga, however, we made a stop in New Delhi. There, we spent an evening with a group of Indian friends, showing our film on the Galápagos Islands. The film's success was as great as that of our film on Corsica, when we showed it in the Seychelles; and as that of our film on Kenya, when we showed it in Tahiti. As a result of this showing, we received an invitation from Madam Indira Gandhi, then prime minister of India, to spend an evening with her. It turned out that Mrs. Gandhi was very well informed indeed on the question of tigers, and she surprised us by the precision of her questions on technical aspects of shooting film. None of her questions interfered at all with the lady's attention to every sound uttered by her five-year-old grandson, who was also there. We came away from our meeting with Mrs. Gandhi with two very strong impressions: she is a very solitary person; and she is gifted with much human warmth.

Shortly thereafter, we reached Kasiranga, and we asked for Dev Goswami. Indeed, we were the guests of Dev, his charming wife, and his three children. While we drank strong tea and munched biscuits, Dev told me this story:

---

*A French fraternal and patriotic organization.

For some time, a tiger had been killing young domesticated buffalo in a nearby village. The tiger's method was simple. At dusk, he would come out of the nearby jungle and cross the fields by walking along some embankments made of dried mud. The dogs, of course, would begin barking, but that didn't stop the tiger. He'd clear the edge of the village in two or three bounds, jump over the fence into the cattle enclosure and seize one of the calves. Then he'd be over the fence in a flash and drag the calf off into the jungle. The next day, the only thing left of the calf would be its spinal column. Things got so bad that the villagers were afraid even to go to the water hole.

Since Dev was the only man authorized to carry weapons, the villagers appealed to him to save the village from the tiger. From the tiger's tracks, Dev was certain that he was dealing with an unusually large and clever animal who had decided to prey on the animals in the enclosure rather than take the trouble to do his hunting in the jungle.

"The first time I saw his tracks," Dev told me, "I knew that the tiger was a large male. His tracks were as big as my open hand."

A number of days passed without anyone seeing the tiger and without any more calves being carried off. People began to think that perhaps the tiger had changed his territory. A few of the villagers said that the animal probably had died. Then, one morning in December, in the middle of the rainy season, a terrified woman of the village saw the tiger. He passed within fifty yards of her, dragging a goat between his front paws, his fangs buried in the goat's shoulder.

Immediately, the alarm was given, and someone was sent to fetch Dev, who lived at the edge of the preserve near the elephant stables. Dev set out on the tiger's trail alone, with his rifle. As long as the animal kept to open spaces, there was no difficulty in following him. His large, round tracks were clearly visible in the ground, as were the tracks of the goat being dragged along.

When he drew near the edge of the jungle, Dev became very cautious, holding his loaded rifle ready. There was an open space, bordered by a ditch, which rose into a small hill or knoll and then descended until it was lost among the trees. The vegetation was not thick at this particular point. There were shrubs and tufts of grass and trees no larger than eighteen inches in diameter. This was not yet the jungle.

For a man with Dev's experience, finding the goat's carcass was child's play. It was there, where he had expected to find it, behind the knoll. Only the hind quarters had been eaten, and the rest was still intact. If it had not been for a swarm of flies around the carcass, the villagers would have been able to use the meat.

Dev did not touch the carcass. He knew that the tiger was still in the area, and that he would probably return after dark to finish his meal. In the meantime, Dev decided to return to the village.

Turning, he saw two villagers, armed with pickaxes and iron bars, coming toward him. The rest of the people were standing in front of the outermost houses of the village, not daring to come closer. The two men made a gesture with their hands. Dev raised his arm to reply but, before he had completed the gesture, the tiger was upon him. Apparently, the animal had been hiding in the tall grass near the goat's carcass. He had not dared attack as long as Dev was facing him but, as soon as the man had turned to go, the tiger sprang.

As soon as the tiger charged, Dev knew that he had only one chance of getting out of the jungle alive. He knew that the tiger did not attack in order to kill him—otherwise the animal would already have broken his neck—but to defend his property; that is, the goat which was his meal. Dev had observed this kind of behavior before among tigers. When a feline is near its prey and another predator comes too near, the cat will attack. It usually wounds the other predator, but does not try to kill it.

Under the force of the attack, Dev's rifle fell to the ground, and he felt the tiger's great fangs sink into his right thigh. An unconscious reflex made Dev reach behind him to seize the tiger's head and plunge his fingers into the animal's eyes. "The fur was so thick," Dev recalled, "that I couldn't even find the eyes!"

The tiger's weight pulled Dev to the ground, and then the animal, like a cat playing with a mouse, held Dev's body between his two enormous paws and began licking the blood flowing from his leg.

It must be remembered that Dev is a man of long experience with wild animals. Anyone else would have screamed in pain and terror. But not Dev. He did not even whimper. Instead, he reflected on his situation—but by that almost immediate and instinctual process of reflection peculiar to men who live among animals.

Dev was lying on his side, motionless on the ground. He could smell the strong animal odor, and he felt the tiger's breath on his thigh. One massive paw grazed his head; the other dug into his forearm. "I opened my eyes," Dev recalled, "and I could see the bone in my arm." Yet, he was aware that the tiger had not begun to tear into his thigh. The animal had simply sunk his fangs into the flesh—and, luckily for Dev, had missed the femoral artery. The second stroke of luck was the presence of the two men, who now began waving their arms, shouting at the top of their voices, throwing stones, and moving slowly toward the edge of the jungle. Dev felt the tiger's fangs being withdrawn

Our cameras are whirling. Less than sixty yards away from our hiding place, this female tiger has brought down a buffalo calf. In less than thirty seconds, the tiger will whisk away her prey by dragging it by the neck into the underbrush.

from his leg as the animal raised his head to roar at these new intruders. The roar was the last thing Dev remembered before he fainted.

He learned later that when the two men had come to within twenty yards, the tiger turned and disappeared into the jungle, abandoning his prey. Dev was then carried to the nearby village. By chance, a truck was passing and was flagged down. The bleeding man had just regained consciousness and was loaded aboard, wrapped in a blanket. Dev asked that his wife be summoned, but without telling her what had happened. She arrived a few minutes later, in tears. She rode with her husband in the truck, holding him with one hand and, with the other, making him drink from a bowl of milk that she had brought. The nearest hospital was forty miles away, and Dev's son, who was with his father and mother during the endless ride, told me: "My father's face was gray, and he didn't look at anything except my mother."

Dev was released from the hospital seven months later. He still limps from his wound, but at least he can walk. He is once more chief guard at the Kasiranga preserve.

While he was in the hospital, none of the villagers dared hunt the tiger, even when the latter carried off several goats from the village compound. Then, one day, a hunter arrived from New Delhi. Since this was a preserve, there was no question of beating the bushes for the tiger. Instead, an ambush was set. A dead goat was hung from a post set up near the edge of the jungle, and the hunter settled down to wait for the tiger. He waited, in vain, for five nights. On the sixth night, he had hardly arrived before the tiger sprang out of the darkness and seized that goat. The hunter fired—perhaps too quickly. The tiger escaped into the jungle. No one dared follow. In everyone's eyes, this tiger was now a man-eater.

Weeks passed and became months. When Dev was released from the hospital and returned home, the tiger was still at large. He had been seen on two occasions—walking on three paws. The hunter's shot had obviously wounded him. Dev now decided to finish the job. With three of his friends—one of them was one of the two men who had saved his life—he began tracking the tiger.

"I happened to catch sight of him as we were walking along the river. He was lying down, close to a large stump. He looked at me, but did not even roar. I shot twice. He died about ten yards from where I shot him. I examined the body. The hunter's bullet had broken his front paw, and the wound was still running. One of my shots had hit him in the eye; the other, in the neck.

"I sent one of my friends for a shovel and we dug a deep hole and buried the tiger there. I couldn't bring myself to take his hide, or his head—out of respect for a fallen foe, I suppose. My son made a cast of one of his pawprints with some candlewax. So far as I was concerned, I didn't need any souvenir of the tiger. I already had one—here, in my leg."

Protecting nature

The study of problems having to do with the protection of species is often as important as the study of the species themselves. There can be no biology without ecology.

One of the most effective weapons of conservationists is accurate information—information that does not necessarily include the kind of specialized knowledge that is the domain of research scientists. Some of this information is essential knowledge for the general public. Just as a child learns that a river has both a source and a mouth, he or she should also learn, for example, that if hawks and eagles and other birds of prey are destroyed, the number of snakes will increase. It should be common knowledge that, if you cut down the trees of a forest, you condemn many animals to death. A forest is the cool, shady shelter that animals need; it is also their hunting ground for the food that they need to survive.

Forests and jungles do not disappear overnight. My opinion, however, which I formed after an extensive study in the field, is that the main reason for the greatly diminished number of tigers in India is not so much the exploitation of the jungles, but the over-hunting that antedates the rape of the jungles.

It is a commonly accepted belief that man has always hunted, and that the effect of his hunting, like that of other predators, is "natural." Nothing, in fact, could be further from the truth. Man, by birth, is not a hunter, but a gatherer of fruit and vegetables.

We have had the opportunity of shooting two films, on behalf of the French Paleontological Mission, along the banks of the Omo River in Ethiopia. The aim of the expedition was to discover, if possible, the remains of ancestors of the human race. One such remain was a human jawbone some 2.8 million years old. This bone gave considerable information on the eating habits of man's ancestors. The canine teeth in the jawbone were very small, while the molars were huge. This indicates a diet of berries, roots, grain, and fruit—and very little meat.

It seems probable that later our ancestors did hunt, using what some call "tools" but what I prefer to think of as weapons. But they did not hunt at the beginning, when their habits were no doubt very similar to those of the great apes. It was only later that man devised methods of fishing and hunting. Even then, man's impact on nature was no doubt comparable to that of the last "primitive" peoples of the twentieth century who live in the Philippines, in Australia, or in the Kalahari desert.

It was not until the invention of firearms and, at the beginning of the twentieth century, the development of means of rapid transportation, and finally the demographic explosion, that man as a predator began to have a really disastrous effect on the animal kingdom. It has been estimated—and remember that we are talking only about species that have disappeared because of man, and not those that become extinct through natural causes—that, from the time of Christ to the Middle Ages, 100 species became extinct. From the Middle Ages to the beginning of the present century, another 100 species have become extinct. But from 1900 to the present time—a mere three-quarters of a century—man has succeeded in destroying 130 species of animal.*

---

*These, of course, are only the species that we know about. There are certainly many more that have disappeared without man's knowledge.

This fire raged for four days along the edges of Corbett Park. In a few hours, the efforts of years have been destroyed. For at least five years, the biological balance of the area will be upset because of the carelessness of a tourist or the malevolence of a poacher.

The death of a prince

The tiger heads the list of over 750 endangered species known to the World Wildlife Fund. There is no mystery as to why the tiger is so near extinction. There have been maharajas who have boasted of holding the world's record for the number of tigers they killed. Three of them claim to have killed 1,000 tigers apiece. There is a photograph of one of these mighty hunters posing before his trophies of a single tiger hunt safari: forty-two skins. The classic tiger hunt was of short duration, about three weeks, and it was an extremely popular sport, not only among the Indian princes, but also among the British. There was hardly a British officer in India who did not bring back a number of tiger and panther skins to brighten his house in England.

For seventy years, the classic tiger hunt safari functioned like clockwork in India. Anyone could take part in one, so long as he had the money to pay for it. It involved not the slightest danger to the hunter, and it required not an iota of courage or skill on his part. First, a group of natives was sent out to cut a trail through the jungle. When a suitable spot was reached, a young water buffalo was tied, by a short line, to the trunk of a tree. A bell was hung around the animal's neck to expedite matters. Then a raised wooden platform was built, above the height of the calf and hidden in the foliage of a tree, for the great white hunter. The latter, armed with an automatic rifle, installed himself on the platform and waited. Absolute silence was essential; and sometimes the wait was long. Soon, the moon rose behind the trees. The only sounds in the dense Indian night were the cries of the wild peacocks and the screech owls, punctuated by the clanging of the calf's bell.

In the distance, a tiger paused momentarily and turned his head, listening. (Tigers depend chiefly on their sense of hearing while hunting.) The sound of the bell came faintly to his ears, and he moved downhill toward the river, through wisps of fog enveloping the tree trunks. Even the owls were now silent. When Sheerkhan hunts, the other animals of the jungle are still. The tiger took a few more steps, his splendid muscles moving under his royal coat, and then halted. The tip of his tail moved restlessly on the ground. The great head was raised, and four daggerlike fangs were briefly visible in the tiger's mouth. The head remained motionless for a few moments, then turned toward the right. The twitching tail was frozen. Slowly, the tiger turned and began walking toward the sound of the bell and toward his own destruction.

Suddenly, the sound of the bell was stilled. The calf had caught the strong scent of the nearby tiger and was now standing motionless at the end of his rope.

The tiger was no more than a hundred yards from his prey. Now, he began to circle to the right. Both experience and instinct dictated his behavior: move forward, stop, wait for the proper moment to attack, move so as to see without being seen—then leap upon the victim like a bolt of lightning. At no time did the tiger sense the presence of the hunter on his platform, twenty feet above the ground.

With a prodigious leap which carried his 450 pounds of muscle over fifteen feet of ground, the tiger was upon his prey, claws unsheathed, jaws open to clamp into the neck of the helpless calf. The calf's bell sounded wildly, and there was a long, piteous bellow, followed by the sound of paws moving in the dry grass. The tiger, intent upon the kill, did not see a long metal tube shining in the moonlight, among the leaves high over his head. He did not see it move slowly until it was pointing directly at him.

There was a deafening sound, like thunder, followed by an equally deafening roar as the bullet tore into the tiger's entrails. The animal fell on his side. The calf now tore away from the deadly claws and, pulling wildly at its rope, tried to put as much distance as possible between itself and its attacker. The calf would live until the following day, when it would die of strangulation and loss of blood.

The tiger was now panting rapidly. Blood was running from his mouth—his own blood and that of the calf. The pain was surely intense. His heart was beating very fast. He recognized the danger, although he still had not seen it. To him, there was only one solution: to get out of the clearing as quickly as possible. By an effort of which only the large cats seem capable, the tiger gathered his remaining strength, brought his paws together, raised his head and, in a single leap, reached the edge of the jungle. There was a second shot, and then a third. Neither struck him. The mighty hunter, safe on his platform, was unable to hit a moving target.

The external wound from the first bullet was not large: only a red spot on the golden hide. Yet, upon entering the tiger's body, the bullet had struck a rib, breaking it, and then exploded and penetrated the lungs, cut an artery, ripped the muscles of the right forepaw, and cut through the esophagus before finally striking the jawbone.

Still attempting to escape by a series of uncoordinated leaps, the tiger made his way down the hill, leaving behind him a trail of crushed grass streaked with blood. There was blood everywhere, on the ground, on the grass, on the trunk of a tree. Along with the wild hyacinths and the throats of some birds, blood is the only red that one sees in the jungle. Already, ants and great clouds of flies were swarming to feed on the blood.

Twice, the tiger half-rose to lick the blood on his flank. Despite his wounds, he had sufficient strength for that, and he licked the running blood slowly. Then, he stopped and lay back, his eyes closed in pain. There was a great sigh. He felt his hind quarters growing increasingly hot. He did not know that it was the heat that preceded cold, paralysis, and, finally, death.

Once more the great beast raised his head. Seen from the rear, the ears were black with white tufts at their tips. The tiger's heavy breathing made them tremble, and his breath now had the sound of a hoarse whistle. He lay there, waiting, immobilized by agony. He did not understand what was happening. His huge eyes, two perfect round circles, al-

Double page following: This is our most frequently published photograph. Why is it that the most dramatic and tragic photographs are always the most successful ones?

ready saw nothing of the circling jungle. Yet, he could hear the sound of the stream running in the valley below. If only he could drink.

The following day, when the men of the safari found the tiger's body, no one could explain why the tiger's head was stretched backward, as though he had been looking for something in the valley.

They skinned the tiger where he had fallen. Two of the natives ate some of the raw meat "to gain the tiger's strength and courage." The rest of the carcass was abandoned.

Today, the tiger's skin hangs on the wall of a sumptuous residence in London. The noble lord who owns the house is very old now, but he never tires of telling his grandchildren how he killed this man-eater, just as he was attacking, with a single shot.

A night, a tigress

"Christian! Quick! There's a tiger caught in a trap in the preserve!"

It was Nadine, my wife. I opened one eye and looked at my watch. Ten minutes after one. When my wife calls me by my given name, I know she means business. Robotlike, I rose and began dressing.

"Come on, hurry," Nadine scolded. "You can't imagine how horrible it is. I've taken a dozen photos in black and white. You'll have to do them in color. Come on! Hurry!"

Taking only a moment to grab my equipment and check my cameras, I jumped into the Jeep and we sped off into the darkness. I was shivering with cold.

Nadine was so excited that she had trouble explaining what she had seen. "Christian, it's horrible. That poor animal! We drove around the edge of the preserve with the chief guard. It was a long ride and I almost fell asleep. Then suddenly we saw the tiger lying across the road. It was horrible—all that blood. . . ."

The headlights picked up the trees on either side of the road. We drove for a half-hour along the trails of that part of the preserve known as Tiger Haven which, it seemed, was a haven no longer.

For the past ten days, we had been the guests of Bill Arjan Singh. Bill is the St. Francis of Assisi of the animals of India. At one point in his life, he made an extremely courageous decision. Aghast at the impending ruin of the Indian jungles by man, he turned over his farming business to assistants so as to be able to devote himself to his consuming interest: the creation of a natural preserve with jungles, plains, a river, an abundance of birds, a very large concentration of axis deer, and several tigers. One night I asked Bill how much time he had spent in the jungle. His answer was given with a straight face, although the corners of the green eyes crinkled with amusement: "That's like asking a seaman how much time he's spent at sea. The answer's the same: All my life."

Bill joined us as we drove through Tiger Haven. I could tell that he was very upset; I saw the barrel of his carbine glistening in the darkness. As far as I could tell, though, there was nothing that he, or anyone else, could do until daylight.

Still clutching his rifle, Bill leaned over and whispered to me: "If this is the work of poachers, there's going to be trouble."

There were three of us in the front seat of the Jeep. Ann Wright's daughter, Blue, was sitting in the back. Dev, the chief guard, was driving. Nadine, wrapped in a sleeping bag, was sitting on the transmission. We were so crowded that I had to hold on to the top of the windshield with one hand, clutch my equipment to my chest with the other, and keep my foot on the running board to steady myself.

We had been driving for a half-hour and I was cold. I huddled against Nadine.

We shot down a long stretch of straight road, crossing over a wooden bridge. There were a few houses nearby, barely visible in the darkness. The Jeep stopped before one of them. A minute passed. No one got out of the Jeep, and no one spoke. The bright red door of the house opened a crack and the barrel of a rifle appeared, then an arm. Two men emerged and climbed into the Jeep, and we began moving along the road again.

Because we were so overloaded, the Jeep was now steadier on the road although it strained in climbing the hills. As the headlights swept the jungle, we peered among the trees, searching for a sign of animal life. There was not a rabbit, not a porcupine to be seen. The animals, at the sound of the Jeep, had hidden themselves. We glimpsed an occasional owl briefly in the glare of our lights.

It was now two hours since we had left the house, and it seemed even colder now. My fingers were numb. But I thought of the tiger rather than of the cold. I could hear Nadine and Blue talking about the animal, the pain that it was in, and the terrible trap.

Dev, meanwhile, said nothing, and the men sitting behind us, their rifles between their knees, were equally silent. When I glanced at them, I could see them passing a cigarette back and forth. With each puff, their dark faces glowed eerily in the dark.

Dev announced that he had only about three miles to go. We sped down a hill, over a bridge whose wooden decking echoed under our wheels, made two turns, and we were there. The Jeep slowed almost to a halt and Dev shook his head. There was nothing. We were at the wrong place. It must be further on.

We continued along the road bounded on both sides by tall grass, yellow from lack of water, and climbed a low rise until the road forked

The full teats of this female tell what is happening. With the mother caught in a trap, her cubs are doomed to die.

sharply to the right. I could make out the branches of a dead tree silhouetted starkly against the sky. Then we saw what we had come to see, directly before us, at the foot of the tree.

"Look!" Nadine gasped.

"Quiet!" Bill ordered.

The Jeep came to a halt. There, in the headlights' beam, not fifty feet in front of us, was the tiger. She was stretched out on her side across the roadway. (We determined later, from a photograph showing the animal teats swollen with milk, that it was a female with cubs.) Her eyes were upon us, although she remained motionless. We could see one of her paws, twisted grotesquely, caught in the jaws of a trap. The metal of the trap was filthy, covered with rust; we caught the glint of a chain stretched over the ground and running to the trunk of the tree. The tiger's white belly moved slowly as she labored for breath.

The signs of the animal's struggle were all around us. In a circle, with the trap as its center, the ground was torn and clawed and the grass had been uprooted. The bark of the trunk had been torn off and the

In the secret lair of the tanners. All such clandestine work is officially prohibited in India.

The skins below were confiscated by customs officials in Calcutta, thanks to the active collaboration of Ann Wright. (Photo ci-desus.)

white wood underneath was covered with dark stains. I looked more closely and saw that the stains were blood. There was blood everywhere, on the ground and on the surrounding vegetation. The tiger had not given up easily.

As we looked around, the tiger's eyes never left us.

It was not hard to understand what had happened. Tigers, like all cats, tend to shun damp, littered ground and prefer to walk in the open, on dry ground. Traffic on the roadway had left two parallel tracks which served many animals—this one included—as pathways through the dense vegetation that covers so much of this part of India's surface. These pathways also allow the animals to move about as silently as possible.

Since the tiger was nursing her cubs, it is likely that she was thirsty and had been on her way to the river to drink, and the roadway provided the easiest access. If she had heard a vehicle approaching, she would no doubt have disappeared among the trees in a single bound and been swallowed up by the jungle. She walked, as tigers walk, with her head and tail low to the ground, her powerful muscles moving gracefully on

Cats born in captivity cannot be used to repopulate the wild. This tiger was released—only to have his skull crushed by the tiger-proprietor of the territory into which he wandered.

her flattened flanks, her hind paws, claws in their sheaths, falling precisely into the tracks made by her forepaws.

There was practically no way for the tiger to avoid the trap in the roadway. It was set in such a way that the slightest pressure would cause the powerful saw-toothed jaws of the trap to snap shut on the animal's velvet paw. No doubt, she tried to free herself by a gigantic leap into the air and then fell back to the ground, her paw still in the trap. By the time we arrived, she had endured this torture for more than four hours—all so that some woman somewhere might have a tiger skin coat.

Before anyone could stop me, I climbed out of the Jeep clutching my camera and flash equipment. The headlights served as spots on the tragic scene, and I remained in the shadows, stooping over and moving forward slowly through the dry grass. There was not a sound to be heard except the murmur of the vehicle's engine. I continued moving closer. Ten steps, five, two. I was now only twenty-five or thirty feet from the tiger. I raised my camera, held it to my right eye, while my fingertips made some quick adjustments. My movements were automatic, the result of long experience—so much so that I worked without the slightest hesitation. My first shot. The flash exploded into a miniature sun, and my left eye squeezed shut in the glare. Another photograph, and another burst of light. This time the tiger reacted, turning her great head until she was facing me. She could not see me, but no doubt she had caught my scent. Yet, I was unaware of any danger.

I moved closer and took two more photographs. I was now standing upright, my legs spread apart, no more than six or seven yards from the tiger. Another flash. The tiger's hindquarters moved, but she did not take her eyes off me. Almost instantly, there was an unexpected and very loud noise. The driver, for some unexplained reason, had suddenly pressed the Jeep's accelerator to the floor.

The tiger, frightened by the noise, made a great leap. The flash caught her in midair, before she fell back to the ground, still held captive by the trap.

At that moment, a peculiar sixth sense came into play—a sense that I call my guardian angel. Go back, it whispered. Go back as quickly as you can because you've reached the point of no return. If the tiger succeeds in freeing her paw, you're a dead man. I beat a hasty retreat.

On more than one occasion, I've had reason to be thankful for that intuitive voice, that silent alarm which, since I reached the age of twenty, has saved my life seven times. Once, I chose to ignore it, and I paid a high price for my stubbornness: eight months in the hospital, with forty days of pain that was so intense as to be virtually unbearable. Since then, I've always obeyed.

I leaped into the Jeep and the driver quickly backed into the road.

He turned the steering wheel to the left, and we crept forward in a semi-circle so as to return the way we had come. At that instant, we had the second extraordinary vision of the night: less than 100 feet ahead of us, there was another tiger. The male had come in search of his mate. He was an enormous specimen, and totally unencumbered by the trap. He sat there on his hindpaws, his head thrust forward, furry cheeks framing glowing eyes, watching us.

Dev, reacting very quickly, made another very fast semicircle. Our headlights swept over the female once more. It was not until then that I realized that, for the three or four minutes that it had taken for me to shoot my photographs, I had been standing between the female and her mate—silhouetted against the Jeep's headlights. My luck had held, but I wondered how much longer it would last.

The following morning, we returned to the spot where the tiger had been trapped. We were astonished to find that both the tiger and the trap had disappeared. Furious at the thought that the poachers had already taken the animal, we spent most of the day searching the surrounding jungle for some evidence of what had happened. Had the poachers really returned, or had the tiger torn the trap from its chain and then gone off into the underbrush to die?

A year later, I got a letter from Dev, telling me that he had seen a tiger in the preserve that he thought was the same female we had seen that night. She was walking on three paws.

The lady and the tigers

If the next generation ever has the opportunity to see tigers living free and wild in India, it will be thanks largely to a lady named Ann Wright.

Ann is an Englishwoman, born in India. She has spent years fighting to preserve the last of that country's tigers. But it was not always so. Twenty years ago, she and her husband were hunters. Together, they killed several panthers—for the sake of the trophies, for sport, and merely for the entertainment that killing animals offers hunters. One day it dawned on Ann and her husband what they were doing. At that point, like so many other former hunters, they became protectors of animals rather than killers. Since then, their rifles have never left the rack.

We had met the Wrights during our first visit to India. We had just

Opposite: Tigers spend a large part of their lives in the water. The newer preserves all have pools for them. It is unacceptable that many zoos and circuses do not have similar accommodations for their charges.

come back from a stay in Sri Lanka (formerly Ceylon) where I had been studying the elephants. The Wrights provided exactly what we needed: an oasis of peace and tranquility. As my wife often says: "After weeks in the jungle, the nicest thing that can happen is to know somebody with a real bathroom."

An uncompromising diplomat, Ann has fought relentlessly for the tigers with her team of Indian protectionists. In their work, they have received staunch support from Madam Indira Gandhi, as evidenced by the following excerpt from a letter:

The term Protection Plan *is somehow ironic. For thousands of years, our country has been a haven for these wild animals. The necessity for such a plan demonstrates to what degree we have neglected our environment, and it emphasizes our new but positive determination to safeguard one of Nature's great gifts to posterity.*

The tiger cannot be protected by isolation, since it stands at the point of culmination of a biological milieu. Its habitat, threatened as it is by man's intrusion and by destructive exploitation and pasturing, must first of all be made inviolable. Our harmful methods of exploiting the jungles, which aim at deriving the maximum of profit from these areas, must be radically reformed, at least within the confines of our national parks, animal sanctuaries and, above all, tiger preserves. The accountant's point of view must make way for a broader and more correct view that takes into account the ecological and educational value of these totally virgin areas. Is it too ambitious for us to hope to keep one or two percent of our jungles as they are, for that purpose?

The Protection Plan for tigers is a national duty. It cannot succeed without the complete cooperation of the Government and the support of the people. It carries with it my own hopes for the future.

Indira Gandhi

The battle to save the few remaining tigers began in 1970. Among those most involved on the protectionist side, let us mention the Forestry Service of India, the National Parks Commission, the police, and, above all, the Customs Service. The total number, however, is comparatively few, while those on the anti-tiger side, so to speak, are very many. At the head of the latter are the hunting clubs. There are more than forty of these tiger safari enterprises, or similar organizations, in India at the present time, all offering to allay the boredom of the rich. After the hunters, in order of importance, come the poachers. The existence of the poachers, however, depends entirely on those who traffic in animal skins: the fur industry—all those who sell, or buy, skins, coats, rugs, collars, and similar accessories. It is the business of all those engaged in these trades to encourage the slaughter of animals; and their guilt is shared by the consumers who buy their wares.

Next come those who indirectly kill the animals: the corporations whose business it is to exploit the jungles commercially, the promoters, the dam builders, and some cattle breeders whose herds are carriers of disease.

Altogether, the anti-tiger forces represent a formidable aggregate of pressure groups. The motivating factor in all this, of course, is money. And the solution to the problem of saving the tigers is also a matter of money. On the pro-tiger side there is the World Wildlife Fund, equipped only with limited financial resources and with the blessing of the government. On the other side we find huge financial resources and powerful commercial organizations working unabashedly at the very edge of the law. It is the old story of David and Goliath.

The first step in the pro-tiger campaign was taken on July 1, 1970. On that date, the hunting of tigers was prohibited by law, first in the province of Delhi and then in neighboring provinces. Finally, one year later, it was banned in the whole of India. At the same time, legislation was enacted forbidding the exportation of skins, hunting trophies, and so forth. Notices are posted at Indian airports warning travelers of these laws. In the hotels, flyers are distributed explaining the situation and asking tourists to support the conservationist program. Meanwhile, the W.W.F. has launched a campaign in twenty-seven countries to familiarize the public with the need for protecting tigers. A fund-raising campaign has been launched, with the support of the government and the protectionist groups of India, to collect over a million dollars. The money is to be used to try to save the 1,800 tigers that are still alive.

At the time of this writing, a full-scale protection program has been developed at W.W.F. headquarters in Switzerland. Over 300 persons from all over the world—specialists in the preservation of endangered species, as others are specialists in the development of food resources or in public health—have devoted their efforts to this attempt to save the last tigers.

In five years, we shall know who has won the battle. In my mind, there is not the slightest doubt who the victors will be.

This sign is posted at the landing area of Cousin Island. It reads: "This island belongs to the birds. You are their guests. Please do not disturb them." The tern on the sign is actually sitting on her egg. She does not build a nest.

2

Bird heaven

The rarest bird in the world

There was once a faraway island, a very small island, part of Seychelles. It was covered with coconut trees and, around its rim, there was a circle of sparkling white sand. Here and there, huge rocks of granite rose out of the sand; some of the rocks extended out into the sea.

As was the case with many small islands in the Indian Ocean, numerous birds made their homes there. Some of them built nests in the branches of the pine trees or among the leaves of the swaying coconuts. Others preferred to raise their families in the holes of rocks. And still others chose simply to lay a single egg on the bare rock, without bothering to provide even the thinnest cushion for the comfort of their offspring.

Most of these were seabirds. Many of the migratory birds had returned to the island every year for as long as anyone could remember. Others, however—and these were much fewer—were nonmigrating birds and never left their tiny spot of solid earth in the middle of the immense ocean.

Among the permanent residents was a species of warbler known as the Blue Seychelles Warbler, or Tai Kiriti. This warbler had nothing exceptional about it and was undistinguished in both plumage and in song. It was, on the whole, a rather modest bird, and was seldom even mentioned by the fishermen of the islands.

One day, an elderly ornithologist, travelling in the archipelago, visited the uninhabited island. Upon his return to Great Britain, he called together several members of his profession and, carefully adjusting his glasses, addressed them more or less in the following words:

"My dear friends, I have the honor to make the following announcement: The Blue Warbler of Seychelles, which inhabits a small island in that archipelago, is, without doubt, the rarest bird in the world."

The news fell like a bomb in the world of ornithologists—particularly since the announcement had also reported: "I regret to say also that fishermen in the area are in the habit of killing these birds for food. The island may also be overrun by tourists, as has happened elsewhere; and that, of course, would result in the final extinction of this unique species."

The press immediately brought the matter to the attention of the public. And, in Switzerland, the World Wildlife Fund made a decision: the Fund would buy the small island.

It transpired that the island's owner was a lady—and a very charming lady, with whom I am acquainted—who lived on the principal island of the Seychelles. She was approached, and she agreed to sell the property to the Fund at a very modest price; modest, that is, for such a piece of property, though it was still considerably beyond the means of the W.W.F.

At that time, the Seychelles were still politically and economically connected with Great Britain, and the Royal Society of Natural Sciences undertook a massive publicity campaign in newspapers and on radio and television to raise the funds necessary for the purchase. Donations poured in and, within a few months, the island was sold to the Fund. Today it belongs to the birds and to all mankind.

An example to follow

Twice, I had the opportunity of visiting the island, known as Cousin Island. Both times, of course, it was necessary for me to obtain a special permit. On my first visit, I found the island inhabited by a young couple—vaguely like hippies, living happily among flowers, birds, and coconut palms, equipped with a guitar but without drugs. Their principal activity was studying the birds and taking care of the preserve. I can say, from my own experience, that absolutely no one is allowed to land without a permit. These permits are rarely given; even for authorized visitors, regulations are very strict. No one is allowed to stay overnight. No one is allowed to disturb the birds in any way—even by photographing them. No one is allowed to pick up anything, not even a feather or a shell, from the sand. There is no possibility of leaving the island with a "souvenir" of any kind. The water around the island is equally protected: no swimming is allowed and, of course, spearfishing is strictly prohibited.

In passing, we must congratulate the government of the Seychelles on its decision to forbid underwater hunting—with or without scuba

This is Cousine Island, sister island of Cousin Island. The owner of Cousine has recently consented to turn the island into a preserve. The plant in the foreground is a pandanus (screw pine) which, along with coconut palms, filaos, and a number of other plants, is the natural vegetation of the island.

equipment—throughout the archipelago. It goes without saying that this has no effect on local fishermen, who traditionally practice their trade by means of fishing lines or, by way of exception, nets. The Tourist Bureau of the islands will no doubt derive exceptional benefits from this arrangement in the near future. On the one hand, the islands are losing a few hundred dollars in trade from the "hunting tourists" (that is, from those great white hunters who kill for fun, for trophies, or for no reason at all). Very often, the hundreds of jewfish and other fishes that fall victim to these pseudo-sports end up rotting on the beaches. I know because I have filmed them. On the other hand, there is much more to be gained in income from the many tourists who, even when they may not know how to swim, delight in walking into the water and, with masks over their eyes, peer into the sea and watch the hundreds of fishes of all kinds and sizes, in all colors and shapes, move tranquilly among brilliant

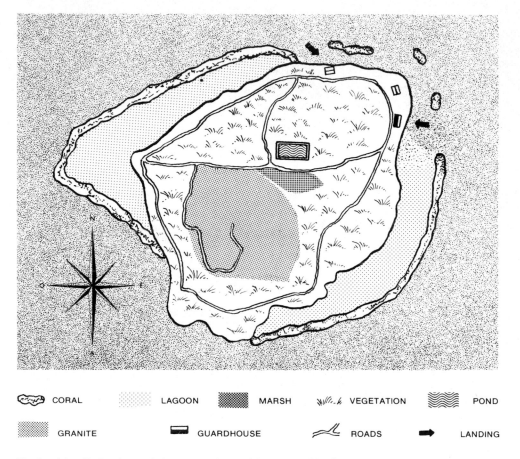

CORAL	LAGOON	MARSH	VEGETATION	POND
GRANITE		GUARDHOUSE	ROADS	LANDING

The first island belonging entirely to birds: Cousin Island, one of the Seychelles.

coral in an emerald tropic sea—the tremendous spectacle of nature at peace.

At the risk of sounding like a publicity agent, I suggest that the slogan "The Seychelles: An Underwater Paradise" is not inappropriate. And tourists may be enticed, without deception, by being exhorted, "You've filmed the pigeons of Venice. Now, come and film the fishes of the Seychelles."

There must be areas of the sea that are protected from hunters, just as there are such areas on dry land. We must have marine preserves as well as animal preserves. The example set by the government of Seychelles in this respect, like that of such countries as Haiti and the Bahamas (where the use of glass-bottomed boats reconciles the need for protecting marine resources with the need for bringing in tourist dollars), should be studied and followed on an ever-increasing scale.

A Texas millionaire on the beach

My second visit to Cousin Island occurred several years after my first. On this occasion, I arrived aboard the *M.S. Lindblad Explorer*, a yacht that can go comfortably where other boats cannot go at all.

It was in November. In the Indian Ocean, November is the season of good weather and calm seas. We arrived in the middle of the nest-building season. There were about fifty of us aboard, all of us true amateurs in the best sense of the word. It was a disparate but harmonious and well-mannered group of thoughtful people from five countries. There were many young people, and many who were not so young. In the latter category, however, everyone was surprisingly active and athletic—demonstrating, once more, that youth is not a function of age and that white hair often accompanies muscles of steel and hearts of gold.

Mrs. Lindblad, owner of the boat, knew that Frenchmen often have a peculiar idea of their own importance, and had invited me on the cruise in order for me "to help the others share in your sense of adventure, to get to know the animals, and to forget Joan of Arc!"

There was a sizeable American contingent aboard, and several of that contingent had contributed to the fund-raising campaign that had made it possible for the W.W.F. to buy Cousin Island. One of them was a jovial Texan known as "Teddy" to his friends, who had the reputation of being a gourmet and the figure to prove it. Teddy was an inveterate cigar smoker. The only time he removed a cigar from his mouth was to replace it with a fresh one. Although in his sixties, Teddy was passionately interested in everything about the island, and his diligence in attending the optional briefings during the voyage had elicited the admiration of his fellow-travelers.

The evening before we landed at Cousin Island, after a dinner well lubricated by wine, Teddy came and sat next to me. The inevitable cigar protruded from one corner of his permanent grin. "Chris," he said, "we're going to reach Cousin tomorrow. If you don't mind, I'd like to be with you when we visit the island. I helped buy it, you know, and I'd like to know what they did with my money. OK?"

"OK, Teddy. No problem. Tomorrow, you stay with me."

The next day, for four and a half hours under a broiling sun, we ducked through low branches, crawled over rocks, and scoured the beaches, our cameras always at the ready, touring the island which has become a preserve. It was undoubtedly the first time that Teddy had been in direct contact with nature. He was the sort of man who was much more at home with a telephone to his ear than a seashell. His delight in everything he saw amused everyone in the group. As chance would have it, it was Teddy who discovered the nest of a species of bird

common enough in warm climates but, for some reason, relatively rare on Cousin Island. He clasped his hands over his mouth with childlike glee, and his utter delight was obvious to everyone. Teddy's entire morning was spent in such encounters and discoveries, and he alternated between cries of admiration and contemplative silences throughout the tour of the island. By the time we returned to the *Lindblad Explorer*, Teddy's face was scarlet. He was sweating from every pore, and he was badly burned by the sun and salt. But he had not hesitated for a moment to follow the group wherever we went.

He waited until that evening, when we were standing at the bar, to

This Seychelles pigeon was photographed on Aldabra Island. The species, like all the other birds of the island, was almost destroyed by the construction of a British naval base. The birds shown below represent about one quarter of the total population of the Seychelles magpie. There are a total of sixteen specimens still alive, all living on Frigate Island.

This tern has never seen a camera before. She is sitting on her single egg, for which she never builds a nest.

Opposite: At Aldabra Island, the ibis has no fear of man—which makes it exciting for photographers.

tell me his reaction. "What a day, Chris," he said. "Listen, I'm sixty-two years old. I'm retired. I have a wife who lives alone in New York; and I can't stand her. I have two married sons and five grandchildren. Look at these pictures. Aren't they beautiful? I also have a house in Florida. All day and all night, twenty-four hours a day, my oil wells keep pumping out money. So don't you or anybody else try to tell me how to enjoy life. I've tried everything. I know practically every nightclub on earth. I've been through everything—alcohol, women, yachts, and every kind of luxury that there is, including some that you probably can't even imagine. But today, Chris, today"—and he looked into my eyes and placed his hamlike hand on my arm—"today, I experienced a pleasure that I've never had before. Believe me: never before. You people have done something terrific with the money. All those birds, all those plants! The screeching and the singing! It was a great show! A really great show!"

Teddy, his head to one side, as only Americans know how to do it, stared into his glass. I think that there, among the ice cubes and the Scotch, his eyes still saw visions of Cousin Island.

A wedding trip

It is very easy to locate the Seychelles. Draw an imaginary line from the northern tip of Madagascar to the southern tip of India. The

line crosses the Equator in the middle of the Indian Ocean and, at that spot, are the Seychelles: a group of dark green islands, fringed with endless beaches and spotted with enormous granite blocks the presence of which no geologist has yet been able to explain.

My wife and I visited these islands shortly after we were married. It was not so much a wedding trip as a film and photo expedition—albeit one that allowed us to get to know one another very well, in every sense of that term, since we went around virtually naked on the uninhabited islands—from which we returned with two films for television.

Outside the charming capital city of Victoria on Mahé, with its columned residences, its women with their large hats and its marketplace redolent of the spice trade of the Indies, the Seychelles are composed of a large number of islands and islets inhabited by extraordinary winged fauna. There are also giant sea turtles which, although they live on the opposite side of the world from their relatives in the Galápagos Islands, are equally huge, slow, and old. There are lizards everywhere. But the lizards' distant cousins, the sea crocodiles which were so numerous when the white man first set foot on the islands, have now completely disappeared. So have the famous dugongs, or sea cows, those strange creatures whose plaintive songs, we are told, so distracted Ulysses. Yet, the Seychelles remain an area of extraordinary interest for amateur ornithologists, and we spent three of the happiest months of our lives there.

We cannot speak of these islands without mentioning a giant nut,

The birds that give this bush a Christmastree effect are called noddies. The birds sitting on eggs are facing into the wind. If an egg falls, it is immediately devoured by lizards.

Below: In case of danger—on this occasion, a photographer sitting on a rock—these birds forget their rivalries for territory and unite to give the alarm by their shrill cries.

Opposite: On Cousin Island this fairy tern is sitting on an egg in the fork of the tree, about ten feet above the ground. The fact that these birds are so white makes them an easy prey for nocturnal animals.

the so-called coco-demer, or double coconut, which is the largest fruit in the world. Coco-demer are, in fact, twin coconuts; that is, two coconuts that have grown together; it will give an idea of the shape and size of these nuts when I say that in French we call them *coco-fesses*— "rump coconuts." Some of them are almost two feet high and weigh several pounds. They were known in the Middle Ages and were reputed to be powerful aphrodisiacs. Maximillian of Austria, the Holy Roman Emperor, paid 4,200 florins* for a single one of these nuts. The shell of the double coconut was used by dervishes and priests throughout the Orient. We were astonished to come across three of them, elaborately carved with verses from the Koran, in a marketplace in Teheran. The seller had no idea either of their origin or of their value. All he could tell us was that they had been hanging there, in the rear of his shop, "since my grandfather's time."

Double coconuts grow only in the Seychelles, and there only on Praslin Island. The trees are the homes of a rare colony of black parrots. This privileged island, this spot like no other on earth, was a temptation that no photographer worthy of the name could possibly resist. We did not even try.

The end of the dodo

We were in Mauritius for several weeks. It was a time of sun and of fascinating discoveries; and also a time of happiness, since Nadine and I were still on our wedding trip. The island is blessed with sunny beaches, perfumed spices, and gracious natives. But it was none of these that made us decide to go there. Rather, it was the fact that Mauritius was the home of a unique and fabulous creature, the dodo.

I remember the first time I ever heard of the dodo. I was still a child. A very young child. I was sitting on my grandfather's lap and he was showing me the pictures in a book. Neither of us had any way of knowing that he was showing me things that would become my life. I distinctly recall being struck by a drawing of a large gooselike creature, with a rather curly tail and a short neck. "You see this bird?" my grandfather asked. "It's a dodo. It does not exist anymore. There is not a single dodo left anywhere in the world." It was the first time that I had

---

*About $6,000 in today's money.

been confronted with the idea that something alive could disappear, totally and irrevocably, and it made an indelible impression on my young mind.

Many years later, something else made a similar impression: among the millions of books that have been written on every subject that can be imagined by the intellect of man, only two are *sui generis*. One is a book on Mount Fuji. The other is a book on the dodo. Both books took an entire lifetime to write. And the authors of both are Japanese.

One can imagine the excitement and interest with which we spent the weeks of our stay in Mauritius in searching for some traces of this almost legendary bird. Its story reads like a detective novel. So far as we know, the story begins in 1598, with the landing of a Dutch expedition on Mauritius. The commander of the expedition, Admiral Jacob van Neck, noted that he saw "in these distant lands, birds larger than swans, having the body of an ostrich and the feet of an eagle." The Dutch sailors called this creature *walghvogel*, "nausea bird," because of its indigestible flesh. The name dodo, which is a corruption of the Dutch *Ded-aers* (round rump), was given later by seamen passing through the islands.

It is worth remarking that scientists, some of them quite eminent, long doubted the existence of the dodo. Georges Cuvier himself, one of the most respected zoologists of the nineteenth century, was led to "regard the existence of the dodo as very doubtful." Nonetheless, many painters of the seventeenth-century Dutch school, faithful reporters of their century that they were, depicted the dodo on their canvasses, and thus testified to its existence.

It seems likely, indeed, that some time at the end of the sixteenth century (probably in 1599), a dodo was brought to Europe to enrich the menagerie of the Emperor Rudolph II. If so, it was the only specimen ever to reach the West. For, shortly thereafter, the Portuguese, who were now in possession of Mauritius, had the unfortunate idea of importing monkeys from Ceylon, and pigs, into the island—both of which proceeded to devour the eggs laid by the dodoes. Thus perished this race of extraordinary birds, many of them before they were hatched.

Today, there is very little left even of their remains: a piece of wing; a few skeletons in Great Britain; depictions on Dutch canvasses; and, in Mauritius itself, in the little Port Louis museum, a stuffed specimen. We will make use of the latter for the opening shot of our film on this extinct species. The rest of the film will be shot in Holland (because of the paintings) and in Japan, where we hope to take advantage of the kindness of the man who has spent his whole life studying the dodo without ever having seen a live specimen.

Mounting an expedition

We are often asked: "How many people do you take on an expedition?" And the next question is usually: "How on earth do you handle your baggage?" The answers are very brief: "Two to five people, and sometimes we use bearers." Regarding material: "A minimum—cameras, sound equipment, kitchen utensils, sleeping bags, miscellaneous" (see Appendix III). For the past ten years, we have always worked with a team; that is, with friends. We know each other well, we accept each other, and above all we all love what we accomplish together. I don't believe in work that is done without excitement and enthusiasm. Moreover, I believe that the people who see our television films can sense the team spirit that animates us and that they empathize with what happens to the expedition and to us during the expedition. It sometimes happens that listeners are more responsive to the process of making a film than to the subject of the film itself.

At the beginning of my career, I organized a few friends into a team which, the following year, was to set out on the "Grand Safari." In order to get an idea of the human element involved—that is, to see how we would get along together and work together—and also to observe our technicians at work in the field, we all made a dry run on Corsica. We camped for ten days on the slopes of Mont Cinto—the last haven of the lammergeyer, Europe's largest bird of prey, a rapacious creature with a wingspan of over ten feet, which has become extremely rare. The time spent there was a nightmare of dragging equipment over rocks, subsisting on starvation rations, hauling water from a stream a half-mile away, and days spent in waiting. The waiting was in vain because we did not catch sight of a single lammergeyer, although we were camped no more than 300 yards from their nest.

From a cinematographic standpoint, the expedition was a fiasco. However, it did teach me to appreciate the qualities of the men who were my collaborators and who were to become my friends. Our primary consideration, of course, has to do with the technical proficiency of the individuals on our team. Theoretically, each of us has a specialty—photography, sound, film. In practice, we must be jacks-of-all-trades. A cameraman must be a photographer, but he must also be an accomplished woodsman, cook, medic, snakehandler, diver, and raft builder. He must feel equally at ease with a headhunter in Borneo, a former S.S. officer in South America, a half-naked Masai herdsman, Madam Indira Gandhi, a French ambassador, the Queen of England, or the Pope.

Personal health, obviously, is a matter of the utmost importance. It would be foolish to depend on medication or first aid in the field. Unless there happens to be a doctor with us, we cannot count on medical aid of any kind—except, of course, for such day-to-day things as cuts, thorns, minor burns, and embarrassing, but not dangerous, intestinal disorders. On an expedition, a spare camera is more important than a first-aid kit. Before leaving, all medical matters must be taken care of to the extent that that is possible. If you're worried about your appendix, you have it removed. You take care of any dental problems, actual or possible. You get a thorough physical check-up. And, so far as you are able, you make certain that you are in good shape psychologically.

I am always struck by the comparative ease with which we are able to adapt to such things as the heat of the tropics, thirst, lack of food, humidity, days of marching through the jungle, diving, sleepless nights. All of these things are easier than one imagines before doing them. It is beyond doubt that when a man "returns to nature," even when that re-

Opposite: This is the tropic bird. The Polynesians use the unusual tailfeathers as decorations for their hair. The tropic bird inhabits only tropical waters.

There are five million flamingoes on this tiny lake in Kenya. Because of abuses and the influx of tourists, one can no longer get as close to the birds as I am in this photograph.

turn involves strenuous physical effort, he somehow is able to summon up the strength and endurance that he needs. This is particularly true when we restrict ourselves to two meals a day (a solid breakfast and a main meal at the end of the day, at least two hours before going to sleep), and when we abstain completely from tobacco and alcohol.

The question of women often arises when talking about an expedition. Is it possible to have one or more women on an expedition? Do they have as much endurance as men? Less? More? How do a husband and wife (or a man and a woman) get along in the wild? And how do women get along with the other members of the party?

I've had some experiences in these matters. When there are only men on the expedition, there are usually no emotional problems. There is also usually no problem if you have a woman—or even two women—on an expedition. What I am saying, in effect, is that it all depends upon the people involved. It's a matter of mutual sensitivity, of common

sense, and intuition. Nadine and I, for two years running, went on expeditions with our friends, Yves and Françoise Coppens (who were the discoverers of the oldest human jawbone on record, found in Ethiopia, along the Omo). It worked out perfectly because everyone understood one another and got along beautifully. That having been said, let me add quickly that women do, in some cases, have more endurance than men. I can testify of my own experience that women are better than men in making contact with "primitive" peoples. They seem to have a facility in opening communications, usually through the women of a village, a group or a family, in the most simple and direct way.

Sometimes this works out in strange ways. When we were shooting our film on the Masai tribesmen of northern Kenya, Nadine was our photographer. As always when on an expedition, she was dressed in blue jeans and a man's shirt. On this occasion, we had set up our tents outside the *manyatta*, or Masai camp. We did not want to intrude on

Terns' eggs being gathered and sorted on Desneuf Island. The photo's publication in 1971 resulted in egg-gathering being banned on the island. The dissemination of information is a weapon in the battle to save nature.

their privacy; also we wanted to avoid the plague of flies attracted by the cow dung with which the Masai smear their huts daily.

Every day, we visited the Masai camp; and, every day, they returned the visit. We were on very good terms. On one occasion, during a visit to the *manyatta*, I saw Nadine watching a group of young warriors very closely as they applied their elaborate body paint. Shortly thereafter, she went along with them as, clad in little more than their dignified bearing, they wandered off toward a nearby pond. A short time later, I saw Nadine returning, her shirt open and smeared with the red coloring that the Masai warriors use on their bodies.

"Don't get excited," Nadine reassured me. "They wanted to make sure that I'm a woman. They don't like to paint their faces in front of white men." She explained that they had passed their hands over her breasts to ascertain her gender—without any sexual intent whatever. (Except in the case of tribes influenced by missionaries, females go beautifully and naturally "topless.") And, of course, their hands had stained her shirt.

Our friends the sharks

During our stay in the Seychelles, as the month of May began, the monsoon stirred the ocean into foam, and, in the morning, the heights of the islands were shrouded in fog. For the past week, postponing our work on land, we had been diving in God's aquarium. Our diving equipment was simplicity itself: a mask and a breathing tube, a weighted belt and, on the right calf, a chrome-plated dagger. The latter accessory was more a psychological crutch than a real weapon for use against sharks. Our limited experience with these sometimes dangerous creatures certainly did not qualify us as experts on the subject. In six years of diving, however, we have never been bothered by sharks—except

Opposite: It is difficult to distinguish the various colorations and hues of these terns while they are in flight.
Above: These colonies of marine birds, like other birds on uninhabited islands, are undisturbed by the presence of human beings. They become hostile only when their territory is threatened.

The meteorologists on Tromelin Island live in harmony with nature. No hunting is allowed, and territories are respected. The result (opposite) is that a man with a camera can come close enough to touch the birds.

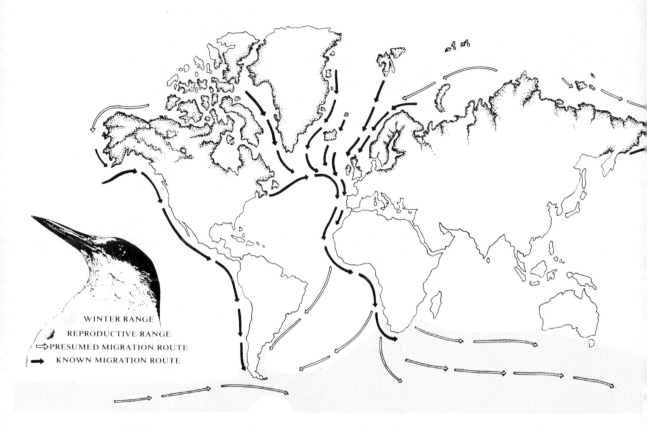

Of all the migratory birds, the arctic terns are the one which, always following the same routes, move in the largest numbers. During their migrations, they feed on fish.

Opposite: It sometimes happens that young green turtles hatch during the day rather than at night. In these rare cases, about 80% of the newborn turtles are eaten by frigate birds. It is all part of nature's way of assuring an ecological balance.

in Polynesia, when we were fishing in the Rangiora harbor and young sharks would grab our catch out of our hands before we could get to the surface. I should add, however, that no matter how long you dive, I don't think that you ever really get used to these grinning, steel-colored, cigar-shaped predators. I have never seen one in the water without feeling an emptiness in the pit of my stomach.

Sharks are rare in the waters around Tromelin Island, but those that are in the area are quite large. Nadine and I saw one swimming just beyond the breakers—a young gray shark—who fortunately chose to ignore us. It was certainly over twelve feet in length, the largest that we had seen. We were in the water at the time, and we followed it for a short distance. Not wishing to become more closely acquainted, we then beat a somewhat hasty retreat to shore.

From what we have seen, sharks venture close to shore in search of

The position of the eyes of the gannet makes it possible for them to see schools of fish in the water below as they fly overhead.

dead birds, small turtles, and fish. Since garbage from the weather station on Tromelin is buried deep in the sand, sharks are not attracted to it—as they usually are wherever humans set up housekeeping near the beach.

There was a story that two men had been attacked by sharks just off the beach at Tromelin. The truth of the matter is that two meteorologists from the station went out in a small boat one Sunday morning to catch some fish for dinner. They remained just off shore, in shallow water and within calling distance of their friends at the station, throughout the morning. Around noon, it was noticed that they were no longer in sight. A search was begun, but no trace of them was found except the wreckage of their boat. Since then, the use of small boats is forbidden.

So far as we know, night-fishing for sharks, using a chunk of meat as bait, has been unsuccessful. Either the sharks refuse to take the bait, or they take it with such force that the line snaps. According to conventional wisdom, in the Seychelles and in Mauritius the larger sharks come up near the surface during the night. Among these is the great white

There are three species of gannets, all of which dive for fish. A gannet has been known to fly for 4,000 miles on a migratory route (the distance was checked by tagging). This northern gannet was tagged and then recaptured, and it was determined that he was sixteen years old at the time. It is certain that these birds live at least that long.

shark, a monster that grows to a length of almost forty feet and can swallow a can of gasoline in one gulp.

Trading in birds

It was during an especially happy-go-lucky period of my life that I discovered there was such a thing as a bird merchant.

It was springtime in Morocoo in the mid-1940s. The migration of songbirds had begun. The perfume of the flowers was heavy in the air, mingling with the dragonflies as the breeze wafted through the eucalyptus trees.

My father, a French officer, had been stationed in Morocco, at a camp at Meknes. The other French children and I constituted a joyous, carefree group. Our principal activity was looking for ways to fill the time on our hands while we played truant from the local school. Our fathers, older brothers, and cousins—anyone who could have made us go to school—were all away, fighting for the liberation of France.

All of us were the proud owners of a kind of sling shot that we called an *estague*. In fact, we each had two of them. One of these sling-shots was never used. It was kept available to be handed over to our fathers or mothers or teachers for confiscation when they ordered: "Give me your slingshot!" The other was used to hunt birds, to shoot out light-bulbs, and to take occasional potshots at Arab shepherds who, armed as they were with slingshots of their own, were delighted to take part in this new Holy War.

At that age, I had not the slightest respect for life. I hunted every day during vacation, which is to say, almost every day. One day I shot at a goldfinch and hurt his wing. The bird fluttered to the ground and I captured it alive, with the intention of selling it in the native quarter of the city. One of my unprincipled young friends had given me the address of a buyer. I went to town on foot and found the address: the shop of a bird merchant.

The memory of that shop is still vivid in my mind. The door of the shop, consisting of two heavy wooden panels, was covered with cages. Other cages, of all sizes and shapes, hung from the white-washed exterior walls. In the cages were dozens of canaries, greenfinches, blackbirds, thrushes, linnets, hoopoes, siskins, quails, finches, doves—and many others that I was not able to identify.

High up in the room was an open window; inside the window was a bird trap set to catch any birds attracted by the sounds, or by the food, of their captive relatives.

I was somewhat intimidated by what I saw, but I was even more curious, so I walked into the shop. Already I had the feeling that I was entering a prison, where the inmates were all birds. The single room of the store was filled with cages. A youngster was filling tin cans with water and sliding the cans into the cages. The merchant himself, a formidable figure wearing a large black hat, was sitting at the rear of the shop, staring at me. The air was an uproar of cries, singing, cooing, chirping, strident whistling, and the beating of wings. The old merchant rose slowly to his feet, pointed toward the cage I was holding in my hand, and favored me with an ironic smile which, I am certain, was intended to put me at ease so as better to bargain for my goldfinch. If so, it had the contrary effect. Suddenly, I was afraid. Like Oliver Twist, I panicked and, turning, rushed out into the crowded alleyway.

I forget what became of the goldfinch I had so foolishly wounded. What I do remember is the bird merchant. His image and particularly the expression on his face, is graven on my memory, and I shall never forget it. I have often seen that same expression since my experience with the goldfinch. I've seen it in Ecuador, on the face of a seller of monkeys and ocelots in Guayaquil. On that of a Ceylonese poacher who tried to sell me a brood of young vultures; an African in Tanzania as he offered me the tusks of a baby elephant; the illegal fur traders in Singapore and Hong Kong; a man along the Amazon who offered me a cageful of half-starved parrots in exchange for a box of cigars. And—skipping over many such encounters—on the face of a bird seller in India who, over a period of six years, has exported by air a total of 430,000 captured wild birds. The cages he uses for shipping his "merchandise" are made of light wood, very long and very low, each containing between 150 and 200 birds. The long, low shape of the cages makes it possible to pile them one on top of the other and thus reduce shipping charges. The boxes are addressed to dealers in the United States, Japan, Europe, and even Africa. The birds are assorted by color—red, green, yellow, blue. I made my way between walls of bird cages in this Indian bird supermarket to the rear of the establishment. What I saw there, on an immense table, made my blood run cold. Two men were standing on opposite sides of the table. As cages of birds were carried past them on a conveyor belt, the men were painting the terrified birds with spray guns.

"The Japanese like colored birds," the proprietor explained nonchalantly. "And we have to keep our customers happy."

"But the paint kills the birds, doesn't it?"

"It kills some of them immediately, but others live until they're delivered. Air delivery is very quick—and of course we're paid before we ship the merchandise."

The scandal of animals in captivity

Unfortunately, the number of birds officially exported from India every year is far in excess of 430,000. And the same kind of "merchandise" is exported every year from Africa, Latin America, New Guinea, Bangkok, Djakarta—to mention only the more important centers of this traffic. The birds who are the victims of this commerce are not only the more common varieties, but also some very rare species. A publicity release of the International Union for the Conservation of Nature and Natural Resources, dated March 1973, listed 230 species of birds protected by the Union, of which more than half are considered rare, and at least thirty are on the IUCN's Red Data list of endangered species.

The situation is no more encouraging with respect to mammals and reptiles. In certain countries, such as Spain, Japan, and France, where there is absolutely no legislation to protect animals, it is scandalous. Af-

This is Tromelin Island. The meteorological station's landing strip is the broad band in the middle of the island, and the station itself is to the left, alongside the beach. It is made of reinforced concrete so as to be safe against hurricanes. There are three colonies of gannets on the island.

ter every television broadcast, letters pour in from viewers telling us about new slaughters of animals. We have suggested a program to the authorities which, in our opinion, is designed to correct these abuses. Here are the program's main points:

1. *For birds:* Establish a clear-cut legal distinction between domestic birds (that is, those traditionally born and bred in captivity, such

Twice a day, the adult gannets return to the nest to feed their young. When they do so, frigate birds dive from overhead to steal the gannets' fish. They grab it in their beaks and swallow it on the wing.

as canaries and parakeets) and those captured wild. The first category can be tolerated in captivity under decent conditions. The second category of birds should not be exploited commercially until a committee of specialists has studied the matter and given its approval. (When I say ''specialists,'' I mean to exclude amateurs, no matter how well-intentioned.)

2. *For mammals and reptiles:* First, draw up a list of rare animals presently in captivity: gorillas, oryx, tigers, panthers, rhinoceroses, vicunas, turtles, crocodiles, polar bears, pandas, etc. The question of defining the "captive species" that reproduce in captivity must be studied, so that specimens of these species may be supplied to zoos from animals bred in captivity. Obviously, it is essential that legislation in this respect be drawn up by specialists who have no vested interest in exploiting nature—which would exclude curators of zoos, circus personnel, directors of preserves, veterinarians associated with commercial enterprises, manufacturers of animal food, persons involved in the safari industry, and so forth.

If we had to summarize our notion of respect for life in one sentence, it would be this: the final word in conservation should no longer be left to the exploiter of nature but to the ecologist.

The future of birds

Every year, at least two species of birds become extinct. Birds, like hundreds of other animals and plants, have become extremely vulnerable because of the population explosion and its direct consequences: the exploitation of the soil, the forests and jungles, the seashore, and the surface of the earth in general.

Still, efforts at protection are being made. In Singapore, for example, there is a valley, covered by dense vegetation, which has become a bird sanctuary. The amazing thing about this particular sanctuary, which is completely surrounded by factories, is that it is actually a gigantic cage. An enormous net, made of steel cables, spreads over the entire valley. All species of birds live in (almost) total freedom within the sanctuary. Visitors are allowed to watch the birds and to listen to them singing, but not to disturb them in any way. One feature of the sanctuary is that, in the sky overhead, one sees vultures constantly circling over the net.

In favor of birds is the fact that they are remarkably adaptable creatures, as city dwellers often have cause to know. It is true that the last wild falcon in Paris died five or six years ago, near the Place Pigalle, the victim of an illegal shot. Yet, other birds, and particularly swallows and starlings, seem to have adjusted perfectly to urban life. Let me give one or two examples.

During the summer, when the roads and highways leading to and from Paris are jammed with slow-moving traffic, there are flocks of swallows perched along the roadside. As soon as traffic grinds to a halt

This very rare photograph was the only one ever made of the Seychelles widow until recently. This bird loves shade and quiet. It is found on only one island, La Digue. There are probably less than thirty specimens alive today.

(as it does with irritating frequency), the swallows of Paris swoop down to pick the dead insects off of the headlights and radiator grills of the cars returning to the city from the surrounding countryside. I've even seen swallows on the Champs-Elysées, picking insects off the grill of a car parked in front of a drugstore.

City starlings are equally ingenious and courageous in finding food. You can see them conscientiously hunting for insects in the impossibly narrow strip of grass that divides the lanes of many streets and highways, while the cars and trucks whiz by at sixty or seventy miles an hour just a couple of inches away. The birds' complete lack of fear is astonishing.

The adaptability of birds, however, as illustrated by these examples, should not make us forget that birds are still being destroyed by the thousands. When ships spill oil in the sea, marine birds are attracted by their reflections in the water, become stuck in the oil, and die of thirst. Migratory birds die after being thrown off course by low-frequency transmitters. Songbirds are captured in order to be sold. And, of course, wild waterfowl are shot everywhere—in the swamps, in pine forests, and on the beaches.

Speaking of the destruction resulting from hunting, we should mention the latest examples of man's ingenuity in slaughtering animals. In many countries, hunters can buy mini-cassettes of bird calls. These de-

vices are placed in trees to attract birds to the area, so that the hunter does not have to exert himself in order to find animals to kill. The ironic part of all this is that the very difficult task of recording these calls was undertaken by conservationists.

As though that were not bad enough, technicians are working on a new device that will enable even the clumsiest hunter to kill animals to his heart's content. This device is a bullet inspired by the SAM missile, which is attracted to its target by the heat emanating from the latter. The bullet, actually a mini-missile, will work in exactly the same way. One can only imagine the slaughter of animals that will inevitably result, to say nothing of the slaughter of other hunters.

René Clair, who spent his life studying, creating, and filming beauty, wrote: "There is nothing more beautiful than the song of a bird." One night, at the Salle Pleyel in Paris, we had an audience of about 2,000 people for a conservation show. On that occasion, we tried something for the first time. Before playing a tape of the morning song of a blackbird, we plunged the auditorium into total darkness. Then we started the tape. When it was over, we turned on the lights. The audience sat there in complete silence, stunned by what they had heard, for several seconds before bursting into wild applause.

Sooner or later, we must choose which sound we prefer: a rifle shot or the song of a bird.

Opposite: The harmony and beauty of nature fascinated us during our stay in the Seychelles. This photograph, taken at dawn, was made on Aride Island, near Praslin Island.

3

My friends, the elephants

Three months among the herds

"What animals do you like best?"

We're often asked that question. Usually, I say that I like them all the same: the giant turtles as well as the lemurs; the tigers as well as the pandas; the albatrosses as well as the crows; even the sharks as well as the baby seals. The truth, however, is that we all have our favorites. At the top of my list, of course, are the endangered species. Our work brings us into contact with the horrible realities of their existence: the destruction, pollution, slaughter, captivity, and torture that these creatures undergo by the hundreds and thousands. After them, my favorites, I suppose, are the animals that I know best; among these are the elephants.

We spent three months in East Africa, studying and filming these fascinating animals. For many days and nights, with the cooperation of the director of the National Parks of Tanzania, we observed their behavior at close quarters. Our memories of them were so vivid that, on subsequent expeditions, we were able to find the same animals. It goes without saying, of course, that we would have been helpless without our African friends, and particularly without our guides.

One December night in Tanzania, we were sitting around a dying campfire, reveling in the beauty of the African night, when our guide—ordinarily a very reserved man—asked me a question: "Bwana, are there also elephants in far-off countries?"

I told him at length about our expeditions to Sri Lanka, India, and the Malay Peninsula, where we had shot films of elephants. The man lis-

Opposite: You can tell that this elephant means business because his trunk is rolled under his head. When an elephant charges with his trunk held forward, he is only trying to intimidate you.

tened attentively, his eyes fixed on the glowing embers. When I had finished, he raised his handsome head and said something that I shall never forget: "Then, with all the elephants that you know in this country, you really are *Bwana-Depho* (the Elephant Man)!"

An elephant charge

The success of an expedition depends, in large measure, on the relations that we're able to establish with the people who live in the countries we visit. The first trail to be explored by the modern adventurer is that of the telephone line, the mail service, and the local administration, for local contacts must be established before the expedition begins; but not too long before, in case of a change in political climate or regime. To illustrate: on one occasion, Michael Laubreaux and I left on an official mission to the Galápagos Islands with the generous blessing of the president of Ecuador. When we returned, a short time later, we were immediately placed under arrest at rifle point. Without our knowing it, a new regime had attained power during our absence.

Most of our *in situ* relationships are with correspondents of the World Wildlife Fund, but not all of them. Chance, occasionally, will provide a happy association.

One day Nadine and I visited the New Delhi Zoo. This is truly a splendid place, handsomely constructed, overflowing with flowers and having a particularly worthwhile collection of animals. New Delhi, along with San Diego, Frankfurt, Basel, Zurich, Johannesburg, Sydney, Kuala Lumpur, and Singapore, is among the places (there are not more than thirty of them) that have done much to demonstrate that the protection of species does not necessarily exclude the concept of animals in captivity.

We had been standing for about two hours, watching a couple of white tigers, when a Landrover pulled up and stopped nearby.

"Probably a guard," Nadine said.

An elegantly dressed young man got out and opened the back door of the vehicle. Inside, we could see a complete inventory of photographic equipment.

"If he's a guard, then you're a concert pianist," Nadine whispered. The logic of her remark escaped me; but then, Nadine's logic often escapes me.

When one photographer meets another photographer, what do they do? They tell elephant stories. Thus we met someone who was to become an excellent collaborator: Brijindra Singh—or "Brij," as we called him when we became friends.

Two weeks later, the three of us left together to shoot a film in the north of India. Our purpose was to bring back some documentation on tigers in the wild—the last tigers at liberty. Our first stop was at Corbett Park, a large preserve which, unfortunately, is not a national park because the keepers tolerate commercial exploitation of the jungle, the pasturing of herds, and human habitation. Nonetheless, the park is inhabited by many mammals, birds, and even by such reptiles as the very rare gavial (a species of crocodilian).

There, we abandoned our Landrover and chose another means of transportation, the elephant.

Elephants are like cars in at least one respect: there are good elephants and bad elephants, creampuffs and lemons. Some elephants toss you about on their backs, and others have good suspension systems and give you a smooth ride. It appears to be a matter of how the elephant is built. Certain elephant drivers, or *mahouts* as they are called, will not even climb aboard an elephant that gives a rough ride. At Kasiranga, for example, there is a beautiful male elephant with particularly impressive tusks who is known as being "rough." There is also a female who is not nearly so well known among tourists but who gives a much more comfortable ride. The large male, in fact, remains almost motionless when the *mahout* gives the order for him to move forward. Photographers and cameramen please note that an elephant is never really motionless, even when he is standing still. I've spent weeks on the back of elephants, alone with the *mahout* or with other people, sometimes sitting on the elephant's back and sometimes on the kind of gigantic wooden "saddle" that is used to carry passengers, during both day and night. I've ridden elephants on solid, level ground, through swamps and marshes, and across rivers. And I can tell you that no elephant is really motionless for more than a second or two. Through the skin, you can always feel the shoulder blades moving, or the neck, or the chest—even when, from the ground, the animal appears to be perfectly immobile.

We left the park early one morning, just as the sun was sending its first rays through the trees of the jungle. There were unidentifiable scents in the fresh morning air, and the birds were just finishing their morning songs. There were five of us on the back of a female elephant.

The animal, with her *mahout*, had arrived at our camp an hour earlier, lumbering out of the fog like some primordial apparition. At the order of her turbaned attendant, the enormous elephant (up close, elephants are always enormous) had crouched on her stomach so that we could climb aboard.

The elephant had a saddle; that is, a sort of wooden platform attached to her back by means of chains looped around her abdomen. There was a mattress (or rather, what was left of a mattress) on the platform, which was intended to cushion our posteriors and our equipment over rough terrain. At each corner of the platform were four legs, perhaps two feet high, which were supposed to allow us to climb on and off this mobile mountain without appearing too ridiculous.

Nadine was the first to hoist herself aboard. She sat in the upper right corner of the platform, and we passed up her own camera case, my case, the large Arriflex camera, the bag of film and accessories, Brij's bag with a Thermos of hot tea (hot liquids satisfy thirst much more than cold or even iced drinks). Then Brij climbed aboard. He seemed completely at home. Just as children in the Wild West grew up on horseback, so children of the maharajas of India were privileged to hunt from the back of elephants from their earliest childhood. Brij sat behind Nadine, and I sat next to her. The guide, who was accompanying us, took the remaining corner.

"OK?" I asked. "Have we forgotten anything? Then let's go!"

Following the hierarchical order inherited from the British, I spoke to Brij, who passed on my instructions, in English, to the guide. The guide then transmitted them to the *mahout*, in Hindi.

The *mahout* checked to see that his cushion was properly attached on the elephant's neck. Then he shouted an order and, using the elephant's trunk as a ladder, scrambled onto the docile animal's head and took his place on the neck, directly in front of our platform. His back was touching my right thigh. He then began striking the elephant on the head with his pick to make her rise from the ground.

The use of this weapon—there is no other word to describe it—has always angered me. The pick is an iron bar about twenty inches long. Its tip is pointed; below this point, there is a hook similar to a boat hook. Some of these picks weigh over two pounds. All *mahouts* use them. One *mahout* offered the following explanation for using the pick: "If I leave my pick at home one day, the elephant can kill me. Elephants are not afraid of humans; but they are afraid of the pick."

Pick or no pick, elephants sometimes ignore orders and do exactly what they want to do. I've seen an elephant refuse to come out of the water when bath time was over, no matter how much his *mahout* might beat him over the head with the pick. The beating has a strange resonance, like the sound of a drum, and can be heard at a distance—punctuated by shouts and curses. In such a case, the only solution is to get a second elephant—a less stubborn (or perhaps a more slavelike) one—to go into the water also. Then, ten minutes later, the *mahout* leads the

This is the nature reserve at Marsabit, in the north of Kenya. It is one of the wildest and most beautiful parks in the world.

second elephant out of the water. Chances are that the first one will also obey.

From the beginning of our trip on the elephant, I sensed that something was not quite right about our *mahout*. He was new at his job. The eve of our departure, we had hardly caught a glimpse of him. And he behaved rather strangely, as though he was afraid to leave the beaten paths. Our elephant, on the other hand, seemed absolutely delighted to be away from the trail and crashing through the trees. Elephants, unlike many animals, walk at an amble; which is to say that the front and rear legs on the same side move almost simultaneously. The giraffe also ambles when it runs, which makes it appear to move in slow motion.

Our aim on that particular day was to try to find and photograph a

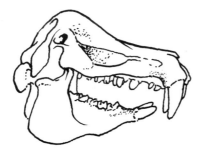

- 35 MILLION YEARS AGO

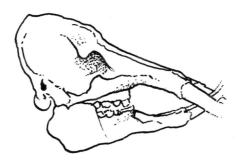

- 15 MILLION YEARS AGO

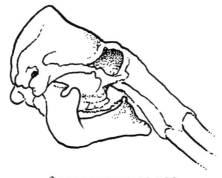

3 MILLION YEARS AGO

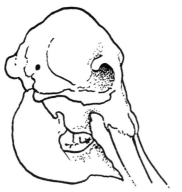

PRESENT-DAY SHAPE

The evolution of elephant skulls up to the present day. It is only one example in the evolution of all animal species, including human beings. (Drawing by Yves Coppens.)

particular tiger that had been reported in the neighborhood. According to villagers we had spoken to, it was a colossal animal. We also wanted to observe the behavior of a wild elephant meeting a domesticated elephant.

As soon as we began moving, therefore, we kept our eyes open, if not for the tiger itself, then at least for a sign of the tiger. As we moved among the trees, we became more and more alert. No one spoke. The only noise was the breaking of the branches which our elephant paused to tear off and insert into her mouth. A touch of the pick on the ear made her move forward again. She seemed a perfectly trained animal. She was aware that the human cargo she was carrying added three feet or so to her height, and she carefully avoided passing under branches that would have struck us.

We reached a clearing in the jungle. I caught the smell of wild animals, but I could see nothing more than a number of birds and a hare running ahead of us who paused long enough to turn and stare at the strange spectacle behind him.

The elephant moved forward a few steps.

"Darn!" Nadine exclaimed. "I dropped my cigarette case!"

The *mahout* had seen it fall. He signaled with his hand for us not to move and to remain silent. Then, by a series of light strokes on the elephant's ear, he made her back up. As the elephant moved, the *mahout* kept up a steady stream of soft chatter.

The animal's trunk, which has two sensitive, fingerlike extensions at its tip, searched in the grass. The elephant snorted, then began searching again. The trunk rose, clutching the cigarette case, which was no larger than an eyeglass case, and deposited the object gently in the *mahout*'s extended hand as we looked on in astonishment. By reflex action, I took two photographs of this phenomenon.

We began moving forward again. The clearing seemed deserted. It was ten o'clock in the morning, and the sun was very hot. Then, suddenly, we heard the sound of branches breaking. Our elephant came to a sudden halt. To our right, I heard the vegetation move and, from our platform, I caught the familiar scent of elephants.

Brij, who was familiar with the ways of wild elephants, had warned us: "Be very careful. Don't say anything, and don't try to get too close. Leave the way open for them both to the right and to the left. But you can smoke, since cigarette smoke doesn't bother them."

Step by step, without the *mahout* guiding her, our elephant drew nearer to the wild elephant. Obviously, she had smelled the other animal long before we did.

I glanced at Nadine and at Brij. Like me, they were fascinated and at full alert. My camera was ready, and my fingers were poised to begin

The African elephant (below) stands twelve feet high and weighs over eight tons. The Asian elephant is slightly smaller. It has smaller ears, and it has two "fingers" at the tip of its trunk. The Asian elephant is the only one that has been domesticated.

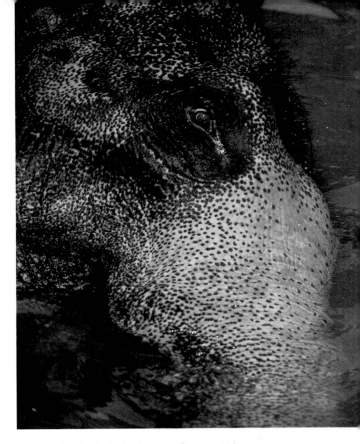

The heads and trunks of elephants, like this one in the Colombo Zoo in Sri Lanka, are often spotted. Like that of the African elephant (below), the eye is protected by numerous folds in the flesh.

snapping away. I could feel my battery belt around my waist. I was strangely at ease, happy. We were still moving forward, directly toward the wild elephant who was now about fifty yards ahead of us. Our own elephant extended her trunk, searching for an odor, for information of some kind. I would have given anything to know what she was thinking.

Suddenly, through the camera's focusing apparatus, I saw something in the grass at the foot of the wild elephant. I signaled to the *mahout*, and he brought our elephant to a halt. Now we could make out the shape: it was another elephant, an adult, stretched out on the ground. I could hardly believe it. Basing myself on my experiences in Africa, I had always been certain that only baby elephants ever lay on the ground. Cameras whirled and photographs were snapped, in color, in black and white. This was excellent documentation.

Our movements obviously upset the animals. I saw the first elephant turn to face us. Its tusks were relatively short, and we could make out a hole of some kind in its right ear. The animal was staring at us, as though trying to understand what it saw. Then the other elephant got quickly to its feet and also turned to face us. A strident trumpeting turned our blood to ice. As I continued to film the scene, I felt our guide moving behind me, trying to appraise the situation.

"Quick, shoot it!" Brij whispered to me. "What incredible luck!" The elephants' behavior was unusual, even to him. "Hurry! We'd better start moving backward and get out of here. They're beginning to get nervous."

Not only the elephants were getting nervous. Our *mahout* was whispering frantically to the guide. We began moving backward as fast as our elephant could go. I saw the wild elephants begin advancing toward us, and the *mahout* and the guide paled with fear. The animals' heads were held high. They seemed nervous, hesitant; but they were certain of one thing: we, the enemy, were retreating. In the language of nature, retreat means only one thing: the proprietors of this particular territory had won.

Our elephant kept moving backward. We were now about a hundred yards away from the wild animals and completely surrounded by trees. The two elephants had slowed their pursuit, and everything seemed all right again. I tried to calm everyone down. Nadine, who is not easily upset, was talking nonsense; and our *mahout* seemed to grow more afraid as we got further away from the elephants. Our own elephant, sensing his master's panic, took advantage of the relaxation of authority to begin moving very quickly straight through the trees and low-hanging branches. We had to crouch down on the platform to keep from being knocked off. As it was, the branches scratched us and knocked our equipment about until the *mahout* recovered himself suffi-

The gestation period of an elephant is twenty-two months. A calf, at birth, weighs two hundred pounds.

ciently to give the elephant a solid clout on her head with the pick, bringing her to an abrupt halt.

At that moment, Nadine thought she saw a third elephant, larger than the other two, standing behind them. "Look! There's a really big one!"

Since I had my eye to the camera, I had not seen it. "Where?" I asked.

"There! He was right there, behind that tree."

"For heaven's sake! Which tree?"

We took advantage of the stop to listen. There was complete silence in the jungle around us. We did not hear a sound from the wild elephants. We peered through the trees. We saw nothing, heard nothing, smelled nothing. We would have to make a quick decision. We held a brief meeting, and I found myself once more in an uncomfortable and delicate position. On one side was myself, the "boss," the organizer of this outing who was responsible for the group. On the other side was he guide, whom fear had allied with the *mahout*. The latter continued to

Elephants, like humans, have holidays from work. They also take vacations and, eventually retire. In any event, the elephant cannot work more than four hours a day because he tires easily and because he needs a great deal of time to feed himself.

jabber in Hindi until Brij reduced him to silence with three sharp words which even the elephant understood.

Trying to remain calm, I spoke to Brij in English: "I think we should continue in the opposite direction from the elephants. Then we'll make a wide turn toward the left until we reach the trail leading back to the camp. We'll take a shower and have a cup of tea. Then we'll take off again along the river to see if we can find the tiger.

Brij had a knack for reducing a proposition to its simplest components when he translated into Hindi. "Go forward," he commanded the *mahout*.

The *mahout*, the guide and the elephant all seemed delighted to do so, and we took off into the jungle at what was almost a trot. After about 500 yards, we halted once more. There was an enormous tree trunk ly-

There is no doubt that elephants destroy trees. But it is not commonly known that elephant dung, falling on seeds from trees, provides a favorable environment for the growth of new trees.

ing across the trail. We decided that it would be better to go back and make our way around the trunk rather than to try to make the elephant climb over it. Fallen trees in tropical jungles are often the homes of snakes. It would be foolish to risk either ourselves or the elephant being bitten by a poisonous snake at this point. Since we had to move backward in any case, I suggested that this might be a good place in which to begin our detour to the left. We therefore moved about 1000 yards in that direction, leaving the clearing behind us until we could barely make it out through the trees. A short time later, as planned, we found the trail back to the camp, and our elephant resumed its usual gait. The *mahout* was now speaking to no one. Brij and the guide were engaged in a discussion of some kind. Nadine was checking her equipment. I was conscious of that strange tension that I always feel after a difficult experience. Suddenly, Brij tapped me on the shoulder.

"Look!" he said. "Behind us! I think we've gone from the frying pan into the fire!"

I looked back. About 500 yards behind us on the trail there was a very large elephant with short, thick tusks. He was sniffing our trail with the end of his trunk.

I had never seen Brij so upset. "I was afraid of this," he said. "When the female trumpeted in the clearing she was calling the male. He must have been somewhere in the area. If he picked up our trail and followed us here after that detour, he must mean business. An elephant that size could charge us and crush us!"

"Even when we're on our own elephant?"

"He'd try to knock us off the elephant first. Hold on! *Mahout!* Forward! Fast!" Brij spoke these last words in Hindi, but we all understood them.

It seemed to me that everything was happening very fast. Our elephant's movement forward, or the noise of the movement, caused the male to raise his head and begin to charge. To an impartial observer, our flight would have seemed somewhat remarkable: in a rattle of chains, our three-ton mount was moving at a gallop down the trail, her trunk outstretched, suddenly oblivious to the load on her back. The *mahout* was lying prone on the elephant's head and neck. The rest of us were holding on to the platform for dear life. I was clutching Nadine's arm, while Brij was holding my camera bag against his stomach. The guide, his face as green as his shirt, was praying in a loud voice.

The race went on. Twice I turned around to see whether the male elephant was gaining on us, and twice I almost fell off the platform.

Opposite: The cathedrals of the jungle echo with the trumpeting of elephants. We recorded five distinct sounds expressing surprise, anger, panic, pain, and joy.

Nonetheless, I saw our adversary coming closer, his large ears fully extended and making him look even larger and more formidable than ever. He was no more than forty yards behind us now, and he seemed angrier than before.

I saw Brij open his bag and pull out a revolver. I had not even known that any one in our party had a weapon, though I may be exaggerating in calling Brij's pistol a weapon. It was so small that I could have hidden it in the palm of my hand.

The male elephant paused behind us for an instant, and then renewed his charge—directly at us. I could see only his enormous forehead, his folded trunk with its horizontal wrinkles, and his two short, spread tusks, looking like the spurs of a Roman chariot.

"Brij," I shouted. "Don't shoot at him! Aim above his head!"

Brij seemed very calm and composed. He watched as the charging elephant closed the distance between us. The pounding of the pursuing animal's huge feet grew louder and louder, and I could almost feel his breath on my back. Brij's first shot ripped through the air and deafened us. I glanced back. The elephant was almost upon us. We were holding on with all our might. It was impossible to get any film footage of the chase. But Nadine, who is willing to risk anything for a picture, raised her camera—and saved herself from falling off the platform only by grabbing my arm at the last moment and hanging on like an octopus.

Brij shot into the air a second time. There was no need for him to aim because the male elephant's right tusk was now alongside us, even with our legs. The sound of the pistol shot saved us at the last second. The elephant, without slowing down, veered to the left and tore into the jungle, opening a path for himself through the trees. I caught a final glimpse of him as, with a terrible uproar, he smashed through everything in his way.

Our mount continued her mad gallop for another few minutes before slowing to her normal speed.

I confess that I had known real fear during the chase. There was nothing we could have done except try to get away. If we had stayed and tried to face down the male elephant, he could have first gored our elephant with his tusks, and then trampled us underfoot.

Nadine had the last word: "Didn't I tell you? Didn't I say that I saw a big elephant behind the other two? But you wouldn't listen."

With the Omo expedition

Yves Coppens, kneeling on the dry ground, gave a few more strokes with his pointed hammer to disengage his find. With the back of

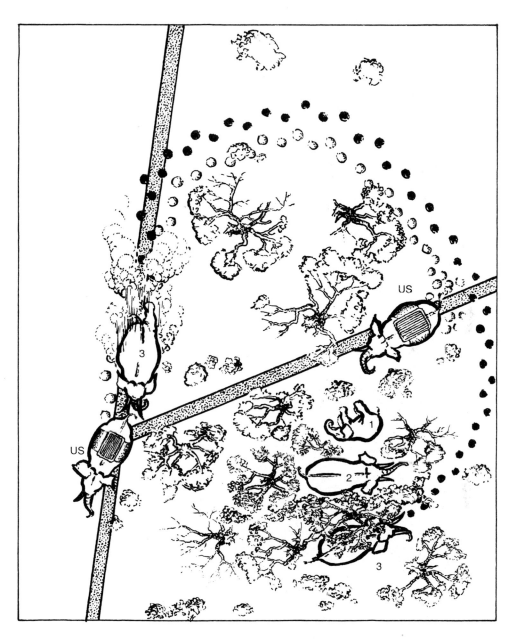

A bird's-eye view of our encounter on the trail with some elephants. Elephants 1, 2, and 3 are among the trees, but 3 soon leaves the trees and overtakes us. We move off the path, giving way.

Opposite: Even while shooting film, we always give animals the right of way. Sometimes, however, we must take risks (above) in order to observe the behavior of wild elephants.

his hand, he wiped away the sweat from his forehead and paused again, cursing the blazing sun. Then he raised his bronzed face and called to me: "Come take a look at this! I think it's interesting!"

We were in the endless desert bordering the Omo River in southern Ethiopia. In the middle of a canyon, which resembled something from a lunar landscape, Coppens, the head of the French expedition, had just discovered a new page in the great book of creation.

It had all begun at the French Embassy in Nairobi. We were there to work on an advertising film. In the course of an excellent dinner, I had made Coppens' acquaintance. At the time, he was a researcher for the N.C.R.S. (National Commission for Scientific Research), and the following year he was to hold the enviable post of Assistant Curator at

The radio transmitter on a sleeping elephant is activated.

Opposite: An old female helps a calf to rise after he awakens. Both photographs were taken in Tanzania.

the Museum of Man in Paris. A paleontologist, Coppens had been trained as a specialist in the ancestry of elephants and, because of his discoveries, in the ancestry of man. He was an accomplished cameraman; and he was a Breton. In short, it seemed that we were destined to be friends. Thus, when Yves suggested that Nadine and I do a color film on his paleontological expedition north of Lake Rudolf, we accepted with enthusiasm and sealed the bargain with a handshake. Since departures on the spur of the moment were my specialty, we decided to set out the following week.

So far as cinematographic and photographic equipment were concerned, we were ready; friends helped us put together whatever else we needed. Dr. Anne Spoerry drove us and our eleven small trunks to the camp set up for the expedition. And so it was that, having left Paris to shoot a film of pretty women stretched out on a beach, we ended up joining an expedition that, over a period of more than a month, was to teach us a great deal and fire us with enthusiasm for the history of life.

Yves Coppens, when he called me, was standing at the bottom of a deep, rocky ditch, the side of which had been cut away to expose geological layers like the inside of a chocolate cake.

When I came closer, I could read success in his face. At his feet, shining like a piece of metal on the ground, I saw the cracked end of a fossilized tusk pointing toward the sky.

"A nice piece," Yves commented. "Now we have to dig it out. But first, hand me that gourd, will you? I'm dying of thirst."

He turned, and I could see his shirt, stuck to his back with sweat.

It was during this same expedition that Yves would uncover the oldest humanoid jawbone yet known; three million years old. It was

also during this expedition, and during our stay at Omo, that I learned something of the history of elephants.

Some 50 million years ago, long before the advent of the present-day elephant, there was an animal now called Noeritherium. This was the ancestor of all trunked animals living in the plains. It was about the size of a St. Bernard dog. The direct ancestor of the present-day elephant, as well as the mammoth, was Primelephas. Primelephas was a monster of about ten tons, and having four tusks. It lived from six to eight million years ago. Its cousin, Deinotherium, had short tusks that curved downward. Like the tusks of the walrus, those of Deinotherium were used as digging tools, for Deinotherium subsisted chiefly on leaves and roots. In digs along the Omo River, we filmed fossils of these ancestors of the elephant family.

Coppens has added a few words to the history of life on earth. Yet, there are many pages which remain to be deciphered.

Life as a function of teeth

The longevity of elephants has been greatly exaggerated. On the basis of present-day knowledge, it can be said that the oldest elephant known reached the age of seventy-five. By way of comparison, rhinoceroses die of old age between the ages of thirty-six and fifty. As Dr. Bernard Heuvelmans has noted, with the exception of turtles, man is the longest-lived of all the creatures on earth.

The relatively short life span of an animal the size and weight of an elephant is explained in a peculiar way: as a function of the way in

Baby elephants nurse between the forepaws of the mother. It happens occasionally that the mother has no milk. In that case, the calf is adopted by another female.

Opposite: Most elephants are right-handed, so to speak. They sometimes rest their enormous trunks (which can hold several gallons of water) on the branches of trees, on large rocks, or on the back of another elephant.

which the animal's molars are replaced. The elephant has molars on each side of the upper and lower jaws. It uses these molars to masticate the 400 or 500 pounds of green fodder that it requires every day—which means that an elephant, in order to survive, must spend sixteen hours eating during every twenty-four hour period.

During its lifetime, the elephant grows a series of six successive sets of molars. As a tooth wears down, it is pushed forward, falls out, and is replaced by another tooth from the back of the jaw which, in turn, eventually is replaced by another. The fourth molars appear when the elephant is about twenty-five years of age, and the sixth set at between thirty and thirty-five. This set will not be replaced. It takes about thirty-five years for them to become so worn and broken as to be useless—at a time when the elephant reaches a maximum age of seventy-five. This seems to disprove the assertion of some observers that elephants live to the age of 100 years.

Depending on whether he lives in Africa or Asia, an elephant's diet consists of grass, leaves, fruits, the bark of trees, roots and small branches. In order to reach the latter, elephants will often break off large branches and even knock down entire trees. This peculiarity has led to the belief that elephants are the greatest destroyers of jungles in existence. We shall see later that this is an erroneous judgment, often based on hasty observation or lightning visits to elephant territory.

The tusks of elephants are actually their upper incisors. These two pointed ivories are about one-third full of a whitish jelly, nerves, and blood vessels, all of which are encased in the forward part of the skull. One of our Indian guides told us that he had seen the tusks spontaneously detach themselves from the putrefying carcass of a dead elephant. "The gas formed by the rotting nerves," he explained, "had caused the tusks to come completely loose."

The record weight of an elephant tusk is over 200 pounds—which means that the elephant was carrying over 400 pounds of weight in ivory. The average weight, however, is from sixty to 100 pounds for males, while a female tusk will rarely weigh more than twenty or twenty-five pounds. It is worth noting that elephants generally use the same tusk as a tool to procure food; most of them are right-tusked, just as most humans are right-handed, while a few favor the left tusk.

From birth to death

In one of the national parks of Uganda, Frank Poppleton was fortunate to be able to be present at one of the few elephant births witnessed by man. Here is his account of that event.

"I was passing near an elephant family, in my Landrover, when I noticed something strange about them. The elephants had stopped grazing. A female and a young male—probably the female's offspring—wandered away from the others and stood a few yards away. The rest of the family then surrounded the male and the female and stood with their backs to them. The animals were noticeably nervous. Suddenly, I saw something dark and shiny fall to the ground: a calf had just been born. I watched as the mother consumed the placenta. The old female and the young male proceeded to clean the newborn calf. Shortly thereafter, the calf staggered to its feet and, with much hesitation, sought out its mother's teats, while the mother used her trunk to hold up the unsteady calf."

Thus began the life of an animal who weighed over 200 pounds at birth and who, some thirty years later, would attain a weight of five or six tons.

An elephant calf lives on its mother's milk for the first two years of its life, but it remains with the mother at least until it reaches the age of

Above and double page following: When the elephants were photographed for the first time at night with the help of flash rockets, they sensed the presence of man and took up the group-protection position (in the shape of a star).

four or five. If the calf is a female, it may stay with the mother even longer.

Elephant milk is thick and very rich. We sampled some in Sri Lanka. It tastes like unsweetened condensed milk and has a bitter taste.

An elephant grows rapidly during the first fifteen years of life. At birth, a calf is about three feet high. By the time it is a year old, its head reaches the height of its mother's teats. The elephant's life, like man's, includes a fairly long period before puberty and an extended period of youth, which allows for development of the brain and therefore for the evolution of intelligence. At the age of six, the calf has reached half of its size. At age forty—just about the time that his last molars come in—an elephant has attained his full growth. The tusks, particularly in the case of male elephants, continue to grow as long as the elephant lives, though the rate of growth varies considerably from one elephant to the next.

Quite naturally, an elephant is most vulnerable while it is very young. It may be bitten by a poisonous snake, for instance. In Zambia, a female elephant was observed carrying the body of her dead calf between her tusks and her trunk; the calf may well have been the victim of snakebite.

As soon as a calf is born, it is protected, pampered, and respected by the herd. The family group is very important. We can count on the fingers of one hand the number of times that we have encountered a solitary elephant during our travels in Asia or in any part of Africa. It should be noted that an elephant "family" is not necessarily composed of an older male, a number of females, and young elephants and calves—as some observers have reported. Often, there are only females, young males, and calves. The reason for this is that a female elephant goes into heat only once every four years. Males, when they become adults, are banished from the family and live in small groups of three to seven individuals. Sometimes we find only two males living together. Only rarely does an elephant live alone. These male groups do not always remain at a distance from the females. It happens that an older male elephant—say, past the age of forty—is defended and protected by the younger males of his group, who are his bodyguards or pages. These younger males are often short-tempered and will charge on sight (or rather, on odor) anything that approaches the herd's patriarch.

As an elephant grows, it learns. First, it learns to respect the authority of adults. As a family moves from place to place, the calf is required to remain on the trail, near its mother, or between its mother and its "nurse"—which is generally an older sister or brother. If the calf wanders off, the mother or nurse uses her trunk to administer a spanking. If the calf tries again, the spanking this time is administered with a branch.

As a young elephant, the calf gradually is initiated into the games of the other young elephants—races, fights, games with trunks, attempts at copulation, encounters with other wild animals. At the same time, the animal's senses are developing. An elephant's eyesight is only of middling effectiveness. It is said that an elephant can see clearly only at a range of less than thirty yards. (That may be; yet I have seen elephants watching eagles flying overhead at a height of 150 feet.) The elephant's hearing, however, is good; and its sense of smell—as we saw in the case of the elephant charge in India—is extraordinary.

In dealing with the animal kingdom, it is dangerous to try to establish an intellectual hierarchy. Anthropomorphism often leads us astray. Nonetheless, my own experience suggests that the elephant is high on the list of intelligent animals, after dolphins and the higher apes, certainly, but not far below dogs, horses, and rats.

I was able to film an example of elephantine intelligence in Tanzania. We were returning to camp in our Landrover, with our faithful guide, Mohodja, when we caught sight of three large male elephants standing in a rather thin grove of acacia trees. I cut the engine and we were immediately surrounded by the sounds of the jungle. Invisible dragonflies buzzed, sounding like miniature dentists' drills. The brilliantly hued birds darted overhead, gulping insects in the air. We heard monkeys screeching in the distance. We began filming the elephants for the pure pleasure of it, watching them in utter fascination. The one closest to us was about forty yards away. His large head and short tusks gave him the look of a powerful fighter, but I had not the slightest urge to test that impression.

We could hear him breathing through his trunk, and he was obviously looking for something in the grass. He moved about gingerly, as though he were walking on eggs, while his giant ears slowly fanned the hot evening air.

As we watched, we saw his ridged trunk raise what appeared to be an orange ball and place it into his pointed mouth. Then we realized what the elephant had been looking for: oranges. We continued watching as the elephant approached an orange tree. It was a rather small tree, with a trunk about eighteen or twenty inches in diameter, but the fruit-bearing branches were too high for the elephant to reach even if he stood on his hind legs.

Our guide, a broad smile on his face, whispered to me: "Watch what happens now! He's found the tree, and he wants those oranges."

I watched through my viewfinder as the elephant raised his massive head. His ears flapped twice. Then, placing his forehead against the tree

A family on the alert. The young elephants are in the middle while the two females, their tusks held in a horizontal position, are ready to charge if anyone or anything should enter their security zone.

trunk, he gave the tree three shakes. An avalanche of oranges and leaves rained down. Without moving any of his legs, the elephant began gathering the fruit with his trunk and stuffing them into his mouth, with every sign of relishing the feast. It occurred to me that any other animal would have uprooted the tree by pushing against the trunk, and thus deprived himself of oranges in the future.

Mohodja was delighted. "You see, he loves fruit! Some of the oranges are probably rotten. If he eats too many of those, he'll get drunk."

Apparently, the elephant did not eat enough of them; for, when he had finally eaten his fill and moved away from the tree, we could not detect the slightest stagger.

This elephant's method of obtaining oranges apparently is not unusual. Subsequently, we filmed similar methods on three different occasions.

The most interesting of these was a scene we observed as Nadine and I were watching a troop of baboons devouring oranges in a tree. The baboons were so busy eating that they did not see an elephant approaching.

We were not there specifically to watch elephants, but to observe the behavior of the baboons. The group before us consisted of seven families and several bachelors, and was dominated by three large males. We had been watching them for several days, and they did not seem at all disturbed by the presence of the Landrover—so long as we did not penetrate their security zone, which comprised a radius of about fifty yards.

As the elephant drew near the trunk, with the obvious intention of shaking the tree, the baboons began screeching and howling at the top of their voices. We had never heard such a commotion, or seen such panic, with the males screeching in rage, the females in terror, and the young baboons in despair, as they began dropping to the ground from the branches and scurrying off into the surrounding jungle. The whole thing lasted only twenty-five seconds (we checked the duration by counting the frames on our film) and then there was absolute silence.

The elephant, unperturbed by the uproar he had caused, calmly took one of the lower branches between his trunk and his tusks, shook it lightly three times, and then proceeded to enjoy the fruits of his labor.

White gold

Given the advantages that the modern hunter enjoys, with his high-powered rifles, exploding rounds, and telescopic sights, the act of killing an elephant for the sheer pleasure of it has something degrading about it. It is difficult to talk about "sport" or "sportsmen" when hunting involves vehicles, beaters, walkie-talkies, and even airplanes to locate the hunter's victims.

According to figures compiled by Professor Jean Dorst, of the Natural History Museum in Paris, Great Britain alone, beginning in 1860, imported annually about 550,000 tons of ivory. This meant that, as the elephants with the largest tusks became rarer and rarer, the number of elephants killed to meet this quota had to be increased; hunters were indiscriminately killing adults, young elephants, and females. By 1880, between 60,000 and 70,000 elephants were being slaughtered every year to satisfy the demands of the European market.

Opposite: My job is to go anywhere with my camera so as to be able to inform the public—among other things—of the suffering of animals wounded by hunters and poachers.

Above: This elephant has been wounded by a bullet.

One does not have to be overly sympathetic, or an ecology freak, to realize what impact this traffic had on the elephant population of the world. At the same time, we must try to understand the attitudes of that era so that we may see the elephant in the light of our own time.

We do not have to go far back, only two or three generations, to reach an epoch when the terms *protection of nature* and *ecology* did not exist. Even a concept such as "human rights," so far as Africans were concerned, was alien. Many nineteenth-century ethnologists, in their studies of the "natives," obviously regarded their subjects as little more than herds of buffalo.

It was the heyday of imperialism and colonialism, and the first colonists began arriving in Africa from western Europe. Once they were established there, they developed two favorite forms of entertainment: alcohol, and the slaughter of animals. Since hunting was totally uncontrolled, there was intense competition to see who could kill the most animals. And the spirit of slaughter grew in proportion to the settlers' astonishment at the seemingly limitless number of game animals. With such enormous herds of antelopes, zebras, giraffes, and elephants, how could it be possible ever to exhaust the animal capital of the continent?

The concept of "biological balance" was foreign to the mind of the nineteenth century. There was no realization that—abstracting from esthetics and sentiment—there is a sound reason for the preservation of species; no inkling that the smallest animal, the humblest plant, the most primitive life form is an indispensable part of an ecosystem* which, as Neil Armstrong has said, is as fragile as it is vulnerable.

Along with the massacre wrought by the white hunters, the Africans, of course, continued to hunt in order to eat. Their weapons were still poisoned arrows, spears, and traps; the inroads they made into the animal-capital of Africa, while not inconsiderable, was nonetheless acceptable because of the comparative sparsity of the human population at that time. (This would all change, of course, as soon as firearms became available to the Africans; just as it did in the United States, when "thundersticks" fell into the hands of the Indians.)

We can only imagine the astonishment of the Africans when they discovered that the white man hunted not only to get meat, but for the sake of acquiring a trophy for his collection—the animal's paws, hide, horns, or head. And we can imagine their puzzlement when a craze for the horns of the dik-dik (a tiny antelope) caused herds of these animals to be killed, their six-inch horns removed—and the rest of the body left

---

*The equilibrium of all life forms.

to rot.* The interest of merchants in rhinoceros horns dates from the same era, when these horns were shipped to the Arab countries and to Asia via Zanzibar.

And last, but hardly least, there is ivory, the "white gold" which the Chinese had worked for uncounted centuries and which suddenly became fashionable. Fashion is a peculiar thing. It is a collective and humiliating need created by a handful of designers, of which men as

---

*These horns are still sold today for use as buttons and as good luck charms. Venice, of all places, is one of the centers of this traffic.

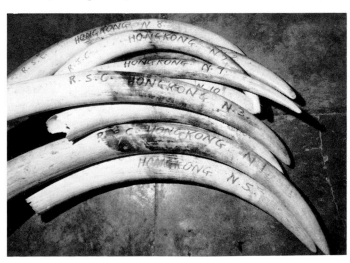

Today, trade in ivory, like hunting, is controlled. But controls have not succeeded in eliminating fraud, poaching, or organized massacres. This is particularly true since China has once more begun exporting ivory to America—a circumstance that has resulted in a 500% increase in the price of ivory.

well as women are the victims. Ivory was all the rage, just as, a century later, mini-skirts or pseudo-Egyptian furnishings were to become the rage. Anybody who claimed to be anybody had to have ivory. The market for ivory was unlimited, even though the source of ivory was not. And so, once more, elephants were massacred all over Africa.

As the years went by, the hunting went on, eagerly adopted by European colonists. Civilization poured its "benefits" into the land of the "savages"; and hunting safaris became a prop of the middle- and upperclass in all the colonizing countries.

The hunters, on their return from Africa, brought with them not only their trophies, but also tales of their adventures on the Dark Continent. Thus were born a host of legends.

The elephant graveyard

One of these legends dates back to the time of Stanley and Livingstone: that of the elephant graveyard. Many people are convinced that there is no basis in fact for this legend. Others are equally convinced that the graveyard actually exists. It is one of the strangest stories of the animal world.

I must begin by saying that I have never seen an elephant graveyard. But, since I'm interested in anything having to do with unexplained phenomena, and since I'm of a naturally curious turn of mind, I've spent time searching for the key to this riddle. The conclusions that I have drawn, whatever their worth, are at least based on months of investigation, observation, and work in the field.

In our grandparents' time, hunters returning from Africa told stories of "mounds of elephant skeletons" that had been discovered in remote areas and that provided fabulous amounts of African ivory. Some accounts spoke of "hundreds of skeletons, piled one on top of the other." Some ivory hunters refused to talk about where they were getting their ivory, so as not to have to share their supply with others. There was a great deal of testimony to the existence of actual elephant graveyards, and it would be foolish to dismiss this testimony offhandedly.

As we've already seen, elephants have six successive sets of molars. When the last set is worn down, the animal can no longer feed itself and dies of malnutrition. The elephant, like any suffering animal, seeks relief when it is starving. The most simple means of relief is to drink water—from a pool, a lake, or a river. By the same token, observers (and hunters in particular) tell us that old male elephants usually live in solitude in places that are located close to a water hole. It seems logical to

A unique photograph: a female is picking up the tusk of an elephant's skeleton. Is this an indication of some notion of death among elephants? There are still many secrets in the life and death of elephants.

Elephants sometimes have accidents. This elephant was trying to reach a choice morsel at the top of a cliff and had a fatal fall.

conclude that animals suffering in the same way will seek the same means of relief from their suffering—sometimes by letting themselves sink into the mud of a water hole, never to rise again. In the Tsavo National Park, I've seen seven elephant skeletons together in one place. Their tusks all had been removed, apparently only a short while before our arrival on the spot, but the quantity of bones was enormous.

There is no doubt in my mind that there have been large aggregates of elephant skeletons in the past, at a time when herds were much larger than they are today. Ponds and lakes were probably the final resting places of many elephants over a period of years. And then, as so often happens in Africa, the water evaporated, leaving behind a spectacle which, to the astonished eyes of unaccustomed Europeans, appeared to be nothing less than an elephant graveyard.

The idea of death

During our investigation of the existence of the elephant graveyard in Tanzania, we witnessed several instances of unusual behavior by these animals. In the famous Lake Manyara National Park, where elephants live more or less in permanent contact with the tourists, they allow humans to come quite close without showing any sign of nervousness. They have become almost tame. Since the elephants' territory in this small preserve is quite limited, we were able to film them very easily without disturbing the twenty-or-so families in residence while we were there.

One July afternoon, Nadine and I were waiting alongside a lake, as silver and as smooth as a mirror, for the elephants to make their appearance. Nadine, sitting to my left, was busily cleaning our equipment. I sat there, gazing out over the water, conjuring up images of the Deinotherium, the ancestor of elephants.

We knew that, during this temperate season of the year, a family of elephants came regularly to drink from the water holes along the border of the lake. Near those holes, barely visible from where we were sitting, was the remains of a skeleton, white from long exposure to the elements. Through my telescopic viewfinder, I could make out a few ribs, a piece of the pelvis, a skull, and a small tusk. I judged that the animal had been dead for at least a year. The fact that it was a remote spot of a preserve, surrounded by jungle and away from the trails, explained why no one had yet carried off this piece of ivory.

At about four o'clock in the afternoon, without our having heard a sound, we saw five elephants emerge from among the trees and walk slowly toward the lake. For a reason that we've never been able to understand, the elephants were within five yards of us before one of the females, walking in the rear of the group, gave a trumpeted warning to the group. The elephants immediately turned and headed hurriedly for the jungle, abandoning, for the moment, any thought of water.

About thirty minutes later, another group appeared. There were six females and two young elephants. They emerged from the trees to our left, at precisely the same spot as the first family. They caught sight of us immediately, but the fact that we were perfectly still—and also, I think, the odor of gasoline, to which they had become accustomed and which overrides the scent of man—seemed to restore their confidence. They simply continued walking toward the water holes, no doubt feeling that they were at home and safe. In any event, they did not seem to mind being observed at a distance.

Suddenly, the leading female stopped and stretched out her trunk. She had caught sight of the skeleton and it interested her. We held our breath as Nadine started snapping photographs.

The animal took a hesitant step forward, then another and another, until she was near the pile of bones. She touched them, then began turning them over with her trunk, never using her feet. The other elephants had followed her and were standing alongside her, as though they also were trying to understand what had happened.

Then, one of the females took the tusk that I had seen and raised it in her trunk, only to let it drop again almost immediately. In silent fascination, we filmed the scene.

We know that very few humans have had the opportunity to observe elephants in similar circumstances. According to our guides, it was an exceptional happening. Another "white hunter" later corroborated our story from his own experience: "On two separate occasions in Tsavo," he told us, "I've seen elephants carrying the tusks of other elephants. And once, I picked up a tusk—it must have weighed about fifty pounds—from a dry riverbed. The only explanation, I think, is that an elephant had placed it there."

For almost six minutes, the elephants touched, smelled, and turned over the bones. The tusk particularly seemed to interest them, and they handled it constantly, feeling for the end and sliding the fingerlike appendage at the end of their trunks across its tip. It looked for all the world as though they were trying to understand why something that

Double page following: The photographer has come too close and this elephant is enacting a charge of intimidation. All the adult animals in this photograph are females. The placement of the calf in the center of the group, and the distance of the second family, is evidence of the social organization of these animals.

should be attached to an elephant's head was lying there by the river. Then, quite suddenly, they seemed to lose interest in the skeleton. As soon as they had drunk their fill from the water holes, they quickly disappeared into the underbrush.

We saw the same kind of behavior two weeks later but, on this occasion, there was an element of chance added. We took the same skull and tusk and laid them at a spot which we had reason to believe elephants passed regularly. We did not have to wait long. Three large males found the bones. The one nearest them came forward with obvious hesitation. He prodded the skull with his trunk at some length; but the trunk came to an immediate halt when it touched the tusk. He raised it. He seemed nervous, troubled; his ears were motionless, his movements brusque, his breathing irregular. The other two elephants were watching him but did not venture closer. And then suddenly, without apparent reason, the three elephants began running away as though they were being chased.

We have no way of knowing, of course, what went on in the minds of the elephants as they touched the tusk. We have no way even of knowing if they realized that the tusk on the ground was the same as their own tusks and those of their families. Personally, I am certain that they did. Do elephants have an idea of death? We will try to find out during our future expeditions among our friends the elephants.

A stroke of luck

People often ask us whether the life of an explorer-cameraman is dangerous. The answer is "no." Of course, there are exceptions to confirm the rule. Certainly, I've had my share of accidents, injuries, and sickness. Like everyone else, I hate being confined to bed, and I dread being in a dentist's chair. And, also like everyone else, I believe that there is a certain star up there in the sky that watches over me day and night.

I am not a superstitious man but I am convinced that there is such a thing as luck, or chance, or fate, or whatever you want to call it. I mean real luck—the kind that can save your life. There is so much "bad luck" and "good luck," in automobile accidents, for example, that I cannot believe otherwise.

Like everyone else, I've had my share of accidents avoided just by the skin of my teeth. At Rangiroa, near Tahiti, it was the open mouth of a ten-foot shark that reached me just a split-second too late. On a boat during a storm, it was a 100-gallon barrel that came crashing to the deck

After the elephant's attack, our Landrover was out of service. The steering wheel was twisted by a tusk, and the radiator was pierced through. But the film turned out very well!

less than two feet behind me. It was a branch that somehow managed to hold my weight on a sheer cliff of the Atlas Mountains. It was a fishing boat, sailing off course, that happened to land on a deserted island of the Galápagos Islands, where I had been without water for three days. And, most recently, there was that elephant charge in India, which, if my luck had not held, might have ended very badly indeed.

Radio-tracking the elephants

Nadine and I, equipped with a special permit from the government, undertook a study of the movement of elephant groups. Our study required a ''special'' permit because our method involved what is known as ''radio-tracking'' the animals. First, the elephant is shot in the thigh with a needle containing a dose of M.99, which puts the animal to sleep

Many females who tried to protect their families by charges of intimidation were shot by hunters. The hunters then believed that they had narrowly escaped a horrible death by shooting down "an old bull elephant."

within ten minutes. A collar equipped with a radio-transmitter is then placed around his neck, and he is awakened with a second injection. A receiver is used to track the elephant through the signals sent out by the transmitter.

While we were shooting a short film segment, which was later to appear in Fellini's picture, *Roma*, we had an interesting experience. A female elephant, who was the head of the family we were filming, suddenly decided that she had had enough of our Landrover. Apparently, the sound of the engine, all the comings and goings, the stench of gasoline fumes made her nervous; she was going to put an end to that curious four-wheeled animal.

A real elephant charge is a rare phenomenon. Nonetheless, this particular elephant charged, and she was not bluffing. At the time, there

Dr. Bernard Grzimek (left), who was with us in Tanzania, offers a brilliant example for anyone interested in the protection of nature. His scientific expertise, combined with his work in the field, were of great help to us.

Opposite: See if you can find the lion. Successful photographs of wild animals require patience as well as technique. In this instance, however, we owed it all to luck.

were four of us in the vehicle, which was completely open and had no top and no doors. I happened to be in the "death-seat" (in the front seat, on the left, since Landrovers have the steering wheel on the right, British-style). My first inkling of the elephant's decision was when I saw a four-ton mass of angry gray flesh emerge from the trees no more than thirty feet from where we were sitting. The elephant's ears were spread (a bad sign), and her trunk was rolled protectively under her head (very bad indeed). I also noted that her tusks were crossed, which is a not uncommon, congenital malformation among elephants.

Without hesitation, and the instant that she emerged from the trees, the elephant charged. She loomed up over us, growing larger as she came closer to the Landrover. It was like a bad dream—except that this was really happening. I heard, simultaneously, a trumpeting from the elephant and shouts of dismay from the other occupants of the Landrover as they jumped to the ground and made for the nearest trees.

I didn't know what to do. All I knew was that I was scared. I raised

my camera and started filming—more as a professional's reflex action than as an act of courage. I heard the film turning; somehow, I felt better—even calm, and more concerned about the film than about anything else. As it happened, the elephant was charging from precisely the right angle for me to get the best possible footage.

I watched through the viewfinder as the elephant grew larger, and larger, and larger—until, finally, I could see nothing but a block of gray. At that point, the female gored the radiator with her tusks.

I had the strangest feeling of being a spectator rather than an actor (or rather, a victim) in this drama. It never really occurred to me that I was the target of the elephant's attack. Never, that is, until I felt the impact of the elephant's collision with the Landrover. It was as though a giant hammer had smashed down on the vehicle's hood. I felt the Landrover being pushed violently backwards, crashing through branches and leaves. Meanwhile, there I was, huddled behind my little camera, still in the front seat. Finally, there was another violent shock as the back of the Landrover smashed against a tree trunk. The last few frames of my film were of a pair of white tusks reaching for the steering wheel, to twist it as though it were made of rubber.

I do not know what would have happened next if Mohodja had not, at that moment, fired a shot over the elephant's head. It is hard to know what it takes to satisfy (or to frighten) an elephant at any given time. In any event, this particular elephant seemed to feel that she had accomplished her mission. She had disposed of the offending vehicle. Turning away from the wrecked Landrover, she walked slowly away, her head held high, trumpeting her victory.

Nadine arrived a few minutes later in her own Landrover. She took one look at me and said: "You know, I can't understand why you're not getting a suntan. Look at yourself. You're as white as a sheet."

The salvation of Ahmed

In East Africa, unlike many other parts of the continent, the regulations of the Game Department are strictly enforced. Not a month goes by that the local press doesn't carry a story of someone being sentenced for violating those regulations—and severely sentenced. Sometimes the guilty party is an American hunter; sometimes, an African poacher; and, sometimes, even a tourist.

The Game Department and the National Parks Department are responsible for the country's extraordinary capital of flora and fauna. They know their responsibilities, they are proud of them, and they have the means to meet them. They are also aware of how vulnerable these national treasures are, and of how enormously expensive it is to preserve them.

The need for money to finance conservation, ironically, resulted in certain "hunting areas" being established outside the preserves, where authorized hunters may hunt wild animals. Fortunately, however, within the last ten years the concept of the photo safari has served to provide a new understanding of the relationship between income and wild animals. A hunter may pay $2,000 for the privilege of shooting a rhinoceros, but the members of a photo safari bring many times that amount into the country when they come to "shoot" a rhino in their own way. Moreover, when the safari leaves, the rhinoceros is still alive and ready for the next camera-toting tourists. One of our friends in Kenya explained it in these terms: "I stopped organizing hunting safaris three years ago. Now, I deal only with photo safaris. Since then, I've cut my overhead by one-third—and I have twenty times the customers I had before. If things keep on as they're going now, I'm going to be able to retire two years from now; my wife and I are going to be the tourists for a change.''

In Kenya, the hunting zones are called ''blocks.'' In some areas, these blocks adjoin a national park. Even though the boundary between the block and the preserve is an artificial one created by man, the animals seem to recognize it instinctively. Several times from the air, I've seen whole herds of animals rush into a preserve as soon as a hunting safari arrived on the scene. I've seen elephants do the same thing at Marsabit Natural Reserve.

The patriarch of the preserves inhabits a magnificent national park in north Kenya. It is an ideal spot: for tourists, many animals. The elephants are particularly large, and the patriarch of these elephants, christened ''Ahmed'' by the keepers, has been the star of one of our films.

There are two things about Ahmed that make him special. The first is his tusks. They are perfectly shaped, and they are enormous. In fact, they are so long that they leave marks on the ground when Ahmed walks. Although Ahmed is not particularly tall—he's not quite ten feet high—he weighs at least six tons; each of his tusks weighs almost 200 pounds. The second thing is Ahmed's advanced age. No one knows exactly how old he is, but my guess would be that he is over sixty.

Ahmed, like many other old elephants, does not always live alone. Two, and sometimes three, young bachelor elephants accompany him in his rare movements from one place to another. He seldom leaves the Marsabit jungle.

The first time we filmed Ahmed, he was taking a nap. We caught sight of one of his enormous tusks through the trees, itself looking like a tree trunk except that it moved occasionally as Ahmed awoke long enough to munch a few leaves.

My first sight of this elephant awakened in me a feeling of respect, admiration, and astonishment. This feeling was no doubt the result of his advanced years and of the fact that he is the largest domesticated elephant in the world (by *domesticated*, I mean an elephant that has been trained as a pack animal).

Ten days later, just before we were supposed to leave for France, I was told that there were two American hunters—Texas millionaires, it seems—who were planning to wait for Ahmed to wander from the preserve into one of the hunting blocks. They were then going to shoot him.

You can imagine my reaction, as well as that of the keepers in the preserve. The keepers and I decided that, as soon as I got back to France, I would make a television appeal on behalf of Ahmed.

The following Saturday, I was to appear on the national television network in France, at one o'clock in the afternoon. The head of the network, Pierre Sabbagh, gave me three minutes, and specified that I could show a picture of Ahmed.

Above: Our friend Peter Jenkins took this excellent photograph of Ahmed, the celebrated African elephant.

Opposite: The first photograph taken of the old patriarch on his territory at Marsabit. We recently learned of the death of Ahmed at the age of sixty. Public support of his protection by the government added four years to his life.

We were in the studio at twenty minutes to one. I was going over what I intended to say when the news arrived that a tanker, loaded down with oil, was in trouble off the coast of Dover, and there was imminent danger of an oil spill.

Naturally, the newscaster had to give the news, and the next available spot was during my three minutes. After a somewhat heated discussion, I was left with sixty seconds in which to try to save an elephant. Needless to say, I did the best I could. Almost immediately, hundreds of postcards and letters were sent to Kenya from France,

Switzerland, Belgium, and Luxembourg, demanding that Ahmed be protected.

The following Monday, I paid a visit to the Kenyan Embassy in Paris and delivered a letter to be forwarded to the president of the republic of Kenya:

Mr. President:

During a recent visit to Kenya, we had the opportunity of seeing and filming, at Marsabit, an elephant who, if not the largest, is surely the most beautiful specimen in the world. This magnificent animal is named Ahmed.

To thousands of people, and particularly to Frenchmen, Ahmed is a symbol. He symbolizes the protection of all the endangered species of animals. There are 288 such species that will disappear forever unless man protects them now. To my mind, Ahmed is as important as a work of art. He is certainly one of the most fabulous sights that Kenya has to offer to visitors from everywhere in the world.

We regret to tell you that we have just learned that two foreign trophy hunters are planning to kill Ahmed. There are two precedents which indicate Ahmed to be in real danger. In 1966, at Amboseli, and in 1970, at Seringeti, two well-known elephants were shot down by hunters who claimed they were waiting just outside the boundaries of the preserves.

We earnestly implore your Excellency to do whatever is necessary to afford permanent protection to this animal. May we suggest two ways in which this may be done? The boundary areas of the Marsabit Natural Preserve may be closed to hunters. And Ahmed may be classified a "national monument"—to the glory of Kenya and in a spirit of human dignity which will earn for you the gratitude of the whole world.

We hope, Mr. President, that this appeal, reiterated by all the postcards and letters that you will receive, will meet with a favorable response.

We also hope to have the honor of being received at the Presidential Palace so that we may, through the press and through television, transmit Your Excellency's decision to the public.

Respectfully yours,
Christian Zuber

The president's answer was received ten days later. By an official decree, Ahmed was declared "a monument to the glory of Kenya." The text of the decree, issued at Nairobi, specified that President Jomo Kenyatta had accorded "the complete protection of the government of Kenya to that elephant, known as Ahmed," who lives in the Lake Marsabit region. Ahmed "henceforth may not, under any pretext whatsoever, be hunted or molested by any person. . . . A communiqué published by the Executive Office establishes that this decree has been promulgated in response to the wishes expressed in thousands of letters and postcards from all over the world, requesting President Kenyatta to protect the dean of elephants.''

The local press was full of the story. "Ahmed is safe by special order of the president," the headlines read. We also received messages from hundreds of television viewers in Europe and from friends in Kenya, thanking us for our part in saving the *Tembo Ahmed*, or *N'dofo Ahmed*, Patriarch of Elephants. Actually, the credit belongs to the man who made the decision to save Ahmed, a man who was aware both of the remarkable wealth of fauna of his country and of the symbolic nature of an animal who, as the Kenyans say, "is higher than the trees."

Ahmed's end

Four years after becoming a national monument, and after constant care by the keepers of the National Park, Ahmed died one Monday morning in the great Marsabit jungle. His body is preserved in the Nairobi Museum. He remains in death, as he was in life, the symbol of the protection of nature in Kenya.

Elephants are born with a coat of hair. At Colombo Zoo in Sri Lanka, our friend Kirivi was fascinated by the hairy appearance of this calf while we were preparing a book for children.

4

The turtle expeditions

A childhood dream

One form of happiness is to be able to realize a childhood dream. For many children, the first animal they knew is a teddy bear. When they are older, visits to the zoo teach them about wild animals—and particularly about monkeys. Then comes the time for a pet: a dog, a bird, a cat, sometimes a horse. The choice depends on a child's emotional needs. In my own case, I chose a turtle. Liking turtles may mark me as a "loner" and an introvert. Or it may be a sign of an independent and adventurous spirit. I don't know, and I don't really care. All I know is that I've always liked turtles.

In less than five years, we've made six expeditions to discover, study, and film the great turtle family. We've filmed the largest known land turtles in the Galápagos, the Seychelles, and in Madagascar. We've filmed sea turtles (known as green turtles) in the Cayman Islands near Cuba and at Tromelin Island north of Réunion. Finally, we've filmed the giant luth turtles during two expeditions to the coast of French Guiana and to Trengganu, in Malaysia.

If we've made all those voyages, pitched so many camps in turtle country, spent so many days and nights waiting for turtles to appear, and shot so many miles of film, it was all in fulfillment of my childhood dream.

Opposite: A young green turtle surfaces off the coast of Madagascar. Turtles surface in order to breathe and to orient themselves. At night, they use the stars to set their course.

James Ash discovered this trionyx turtle in Lake Rudolf. Unlike land turtles, marine turtles are sometimes dangerous. They can snap off a finger in a single bite.

With Gilberto Moncayo

As chance would have it, the first Galápagos land turtle I saw through my viewfinder was an unusually large specimen. We had climbed up a muddy trail to the highest point of Santa Cruz. Gilberto Moncayo, the son and grandson of poachers, and himself a poacher at that time, was with me. We had been walking for four hours, with three donkeys carrying equipment through woods and marshes. Finally, Gilberto halted.

"*No es leche,*" he declared. "She's not far off."

Before us, there was a clearing, surrounded by dead trees. According to Gilberto, a very large turtle came here to graze on the tender young grass growing in the clearing.

We sat down and waited. One hour passed, and nothing happened.

I grew a little impatient and wondered whether we should look around the area to see if we could find the turtle. The problem was that, if we found it and frightened it, it would withdraw its head and legs and leave me to film a motionless shell. Film requires life and motion, not artificial "scenery." So there was nothing for me to do but sit there, chewing a piece of grass and watching leaves move in the breeze.

I had looked around the clearing for the hundredth time. My attention, for the moment, was fixed on a tiny lizard that had just walked over my right foot. I felt Gilberto's hand on my arm.

"*Aqui!*" he whispered. "*El animal!*"

Less than twenty yards away, beautiful as an antique sculpture, was a giant turtle. As though by magic, it had suddenly appeared at the edge of the clearing and was now peacefully munching the grass. I was astonished by the animal's size. Later, I took the exact measurements. The paws were two feet, two inches in diameter; the shell, eight feet, ten inches!

The giant turtle Jonathan during his visit to Nairobi. A native of the Seychelles, he is completely tame and now lives in the Mulhouse Zoo in northern France. Since Jonathan was captured at birth, he has been undoubtedly better off in the artificial environment provided by the zoo.

For over an hour, this old grandmother turtle—I concluded that she was a female from the open shape of her shell—nibbled at the grass, turning her head sideways so as better to be able to cut it with her beak-shaped mouth. At that time of the year, grass was particularly abundant because of the heavy rainfall.

From time to time, the turtle raised her head and stared at us with her small, maroon eyes circled in white. By crawling through the grass and mud, we finally came to within ten feet of her. At that, she raised her head again on her reptilian neck and, with her mouth half open, made a hoarse, hissing noise. Then, remaining absolutely motionless, she stared at us.

I lay down on the ground in an attempt to make myself as inconspicuous as possible. I was surprised to see Gilberto get to his feet and turn toward me.

"Get up," he said. "She's blind."

The travels of a grandmother

The fact that we may have new ideas on animals in captivity does not mean that we can afford to ignore the past.

There have been zoos and circuses for many years in all parts of the world. In some cases, it is possible for these institutions to buy, sell, and exchange animals among themselves so as to renew their supply without having to resort to capturing wild animals. We had some experience with this system while we were in Kenya.* James Ash, director of the

*Kenya has now forbidden hunting throughout the country. Kenya is the first African nation to take this step.

Above: These African poachers work for turtle soup merchants. They use an ax to open the turtles. The meat will be dried and then shipped to Germany.
Opposite: At Tromelin Island, the calcium from this skeleton will make the vegetation at this spot grow taller than elsewhere on the island.

Nairobi Snake Park, offered us a turtle that had been born in captivity: a giant from the Seychelles. I immediately telegraphed the director of the Mulhouse Zoo, in France, and got the following reply: "OK. Bring the turtle."

The only problem was flying the turtle from Nairobi to Paris. I may have been guilty of misrepresentation in my conversation with the airline in question.

"I want to fly a turtle to Paris," I said. "Can you tell me how to go about it?"

"There's no problem," I was told. "Just carry it aboard with you. I'll tell the captain about it beforehand." Despite the size of the case ($40'' \times 48'' \times 54''$) and its weight (220 lbs.), Jonathan, as we baptized the turtle, made the trip without undue difficulty and in total silence. Today, he is a source of great pleasure to thousands of children at the zoo. His offspring will live until the year 2270.

The smallest paradise on earth

Maps have always fascinated me. How many hours I've spent, while teachers of history or mathematics struggled in vain for my attention, with an atlas open on my lap, planning fabulous voyages. Even during recess, while everyone else was playing ball or smoking in the locker room, I remember poring over my geography books. At that time of my life, the whole world seemed to be there, waiting for me. There was no spot so remote, no jungle so impenetrable, no desert so vast, that I could not reach it without the slightest difficulty. To go from Paris to the Sahara, you simply moved southward until you reached Tamanrasset. To get to the jungles of Borneo, you followed a horizontal line to Malaysia; then get a boat, and you're there. Exploring the Amazon was just a matter of deciding to do it.

I had noticed that the world, at least according to the maps, was a constellation of magical, exotic names: Zanzibar, Galapagos, Tahiti, Midway, Maldives, Celebes, Easter Island—all names calculated to conjure up visions in a young mind.

I remember wondering whether there were as many human beings in all those places as there were in Paris. It was not until later that I realized, population explosion or not, that a name on a map is not a measure of reality. A black dot does not necessarily mean that the spot is crawling with humans. A city may consist of a dozen wooden huts. A river may be a trickle of water. An island may be a sandbar. Tromelin Island, for example, is a tiny bit of land north of Réunion, lost in the waves of the Indian Ocean, although it does have a sizeable population of frigate birds, terns, gannets, and other migratory birds. And, in the proper season, dozens of sea turtles come to Tromelin to lay their eggs. It was this latter fact that drew us to that dot in the sea.

We left Réunion at seven o'clock in the morning. At 3,500 feet above the ocean, our pilot was very confident. "It's great weather," he assured us. "Don't worry. We can't miss it!"

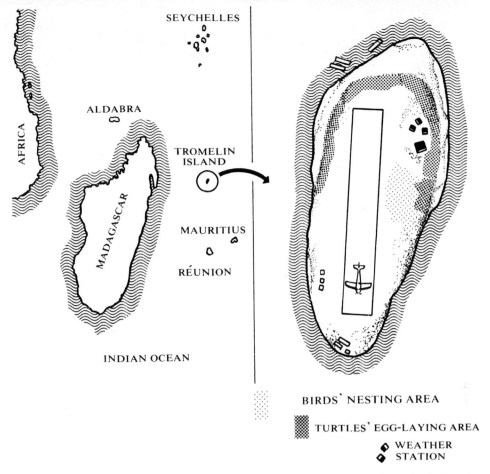

SEYCHELLES

ALDABRA

AFRICA

MADAGASCAR

TROMELIN ISLAND

MAURITIUS

RÉUNION

INDIAN OCEAN

BIRDS' NESTING AREA

TURTLES' EGG-LAYING AREA

WEATHER STATION

Tromelin Island is the smallest inhabited island in the world. It is also a refuge for marine birds and sea turtles as well as meteorologists.

A few minutes later, Tromelin did indeed appear before us. We saw the landing strip: a straight line running practically the entire length of the island. There were a few patches of shrubbery, two rectangular buildings, and a flag fluttering in the wind. The foaming waves framed it like white rose petals, protecting the fragile spit of sand from the immensity of the sea.

As we approached the strip, I glimpsed four human shapes on the ground, waving us in.

"I'm going to circle before coming in for a landing," the pilot said. "I want to make sure there are no turtles on the runway."

Tromelin is a meteorological outpost, a substation of the main station on Réunion. Teams of three to five men relieve one another every four months. Their work, in conjunction with that of such outposts throughout the world, is what makes it possible for airplanes to fly.

Tromelin is the smallest inhabited island in the world. Visitors are rare. My plans were to stay for ten days to film and photograph the animals, the movements and formations of the clouds, and the daily routine of the four meteorologists at the station.

Some turtles, after laying their eggs, are disoriented by sea mist and try to reach the ocean by crossing the entire island. No turtle has ever succeeded. After a half-day of strenuous effort, the sun scorches their lungs and they die a hundred yards from the sea.

The laying season

The night of our arrival, I planned to film the turtles laying eggs. I had already shot sequences of this phenomenon elsewhere, but I needed some more film to finish work on a short segment on sea turtles.

Contracts for filming are very definite about one thing: the footage sold cannot be used in any other film, except in certain unusual cases. Aside from the legal problems involved in using the same footage more than once, there is the necessity of putting together a good show, and the fact is that viewers usually know when they've seen a particular scene in another film. So, I always get new footage rather than splice old footage into a new film. Generally, the new film is of higher quality than the old—probably because by the time I shoot the new film, I've learned from experience. I was therefore optimistic about the turtles of Tromelin Island. I had little idea of what was in store for me.

I headed for the beach with the chief of the substation, Petit de la Rodhiére, and his assistant, Legros. It was a few minutes before midnight. The full moon was high in the sky, and the sand was bathed in a silvery light. The sea was calm, and the occasional waves that reached the shore broke gently at our feet.

We could see turtle tracks in the sand, leading from the high-water line to the tops of the dunes. From there, they led into the large-leafed shrubbery and to the craterlike nests where the turtles lay their eggs. The tracks, however, were not fresh. We would have to wait for high tide.

We stretched out on a slight rise in the sand. Petit and Legros lighted cigarettes. Since I am a nonsmoker, I found equal pleasure in watching the stars as I lay on my back, my hands clasped under my head, the warmth of the sand seeping through my clothing.

The first turtle arrived an hour later. Even before we saw her, we heard the sound of her heavy shell knocking against the rocks. At that point, cigarettes were extinguished and we lay on our stomachs, watching.

Sea turtles come ashore to lay their eggs at least once every two years. Only the females leave the water, and they come ashore only in one place, which is the same island on which they themselves were hatched. Archie Carr, a specialist in green turtles, has demonstrated that sea turtles are invariably faithful to their laying grounds.

This does not mean that the turtles spend the rest of their time in the neighboring waters. They may travel great distances in search of the marine grass that is their staple food. Also, sea currents carry turtles for many miles. Some turtles have been tagged, turned loose, and recovered almost 2,000 miles from the island where they were hatched.

Sea turtles mate in the water or near the surface. The males, who are usually larger and stronger than the females, chase the females until they are able to mount them. The act of copulation often takes place before a circle of other males who are waiting their turns. We've never seen a female who appeared to be willing to copulate. The male sea turtle, like the male land turtle, apparently must force the female to mate.

The eggs develop inside the female and, as the expectant mother feels the time for laying draw near, she begins the journey back to her island. How does she find her way? This question, like that of the migration of birds, is one of the most interesting issues in the animal kingdom.

Let us begin by saying that there is instinct, the memory of a place, and that sense of direction which, in humans, has often been lost. Experiments have proved (by outfitting sea turtles with dark glasses that render them temporarily sightless) that turtles navigate by the stars at night and by the sun during the day.

We've often observed turtles while we were swimming and boating, without disturbing them. We're quite certain that these creatures

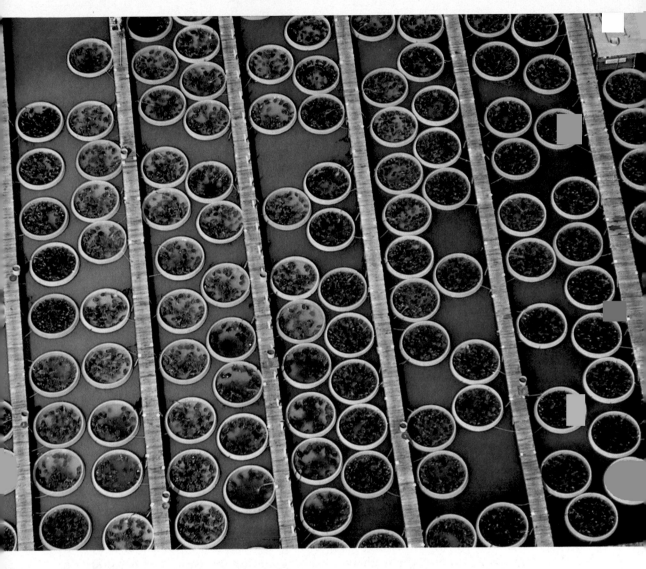

This is the turtle farm at Grand Cayman. Twice a day, the turtles are fed fish, grass, and vitamins. The results of this interesting experiment are still secret.

swim for hours on end and follow a set course. Even if they encounter an island where all the conditions are favorable for laying eggs, they ignore it and continue their journey to the island where they were born.

Once they reach the island, they do not rush ashore. We've seen turtles, on dark nights in the middle of the laying season, floating on the surface of the water offshore, beyond the breakers, looking around carefully before allowing themselves to be carried to shore by the waves.

Young turtles, when they go to sleep at night, fold their fore-paws over the tops of their shells to protect themselves from small predators.

The ordeal

When the turtle reached the beach, she gave a long, hissing sigh. We could hear it from where we were lying. We saw the turtle's damp shell glistening in the moonlight. It looked like a rock protruding from the sand. Then, her head held forward, the turtle rose and, using her paddle-shaped feet, she began dragging herself forward. After three or four steps, the turtle halted. She was still on the part of the beach washed by the incoming tide. The animal, accustomed as she was to moving about easily in the water, was feeling the weight of her body on land. The overland journey of a sea turtle is a debilitating ordeal. Slowly, the turtle moved forward, leaving behind a track in the sand like that of a tank.

Filming the progress of a turtle to the nest is a delicate undertaking. The least noise, the dimmest ray of light may frighten her and cause her to turn and head back toward the water. In such a case, she would un-doubtedly return later; perhaps in a few hours, perhaps in ten days.

When the turtle reached the spot in which she would lay her eggs, she began digging. We approached as quietly as we could. Kneeling in the sand five or six feet away from her, we watched her hind paws mov-ing in the sand, and I got the camera ready. "Turn on the flashlight," I whispered.

The light blinded us. The turtle stopped digging, hesitated, then re-sumed her work.

At that moment, the sand flies, awakened by the brilliant moonlight, attacked us. At first, there were fewer than a hundred of them. By the time the turtle had finished laying her eggs, there must have been a million flies. They were everywhere: in our eyes, our mouths, on the camera.

As soon as the turtle began laying her eggs—which look like shiny ping pong balls—we began moving around with our equipment so as to get some background footage and also to shoot the turtle from various angles.

Like many marine animals, sea turtles shed tears. They are not tears of sorrow or pain, but of protection. In salt water, they serve to protect the turtle's eyes. On land, they prevent the crystalline from drying out. If turtles did not shed tears, they would lose their eyesight.

We watched the eggs falling into the nest in the sand. Sometimes they emerged from the turtle's body singly, sometimes in pairs. Turtle eggs, when first laid, are soft. The shell hardens in less than ten minutes. When all the eggs were laid, the exhausted mother turtle began to cover them with sand. First she worked with her hind paws, then with her forepaws, throwing around large amounts of sand—much of which landed on our camera.

Then it was time for her to return to the sea. On most islands, this involves little more than turning around and heading downhill. Not so on Tromelin Island. At the spot where our turtle laid her eggs, the island is over 600 yards wide. If, after a turtle has laid her eggs, a breeze begins blowing from the other side of the island, or if she cannot see the luminescence of the sea, she may well begin moving toward the far side of the island in order to find the ocean. The exhausted animal will drag herself over the sand for hours. By dawn, she will have reached the halfway mark in her journey, with at least three hours still ahead of her. Most of them never make it. The heat of the sun through their shells scorches their lungs before midday. Petit and Legros have often found turtles in distress and dragged them into the water. "Sometimes," Petit told me, "it's too late. But I think that every year we must save about a hundred of them. Now you know why the airplane has to make a circle around the landing strip before it lands."

A turtle farm

For the third time, the stewardess handed me a plastic glass half filled with an orange liquid. We had taken off from Miami an hour before. It was hot. Very hot. Everyone drank. Some of the passengers were concentrating on whiskey, some on champagne. Nadine and I never drink alcohol; and the alternative was this liquid, with a vaguely phar-

All the turtles at the Grand Cayman farm are tagged. In studying the weight increase of turtles, specialists have discovered that turtles in captivity grow three times faster than turtles at large.

Opposite: Epidemics are the nightmare of turtle breeders. Sick turtles are treated with tincture of methylene. The commercial exploitation of marine life is still in the experimental stage.

maceutical taste to it, which was euphemistically referred to as "orange juice."

We were on our way to Grand Cayman where, like the heron in the fable, we would often long for a glass of the stuff that we now drank with such little appreciation. The tourist brochures expand on the delights of the Grand Cayman sun, without mentioning its incredible heat. It is possible literally to fry an egg on the hood of a car. Fortunately, there is air-conditioning, and the people in charge of the turtle farm that we were going to visit were friends of ours.

We had been invited to spend two weeks at the farm, which, we hoped, might be the first step toward saving sea turtles from extinction. The basic idea was simple: to raise turtles like other domestic animals, for their meat. In practice, however, there were problems.

Seen from the air, the turtle farm is quite striking. It is situated along a rocky ridge, where the jade and emerald hues of the sea fade into the snowy foam of the surf. There are hundreds of turtle ponds, all grouped around a large central basin. There are several coconut palms, and a few trails of white coral. From the air, a sharp eye can distinguish dark points in the ponds: turtles.

The turtles at the farm are hatched from eggs gathered in the wild. The eggs are then transported by air from Surinam to Grand Cayman and carefully buried in sand until they hatch. The newborn turtles are fed sea grass, corn, and fish. They will remain in the pools until they are five years old. At that point, they will be killed (by means of electric shock), canned, and sold in the United States.

Not all the turtles are killed. One-third of them are released in the same spot that their eggs were found. They are set free at night, to enable them to reach the water without being devoured by predators.

This method, if generally adopted, would make it possible to do away with the poaching which supplies meat to the turtle soup factories of Great Britain and Germany. It would also spare thousands of turtles the interminable agony of a slow death. Only the cartilage binding the tops and bottoms of the shells is cut away with a knife, while the turtle is still alive. The turtle is then left to die, and the sun-dried cartilages are sold to the factories.

There are about 100,000 beautiful green turtles on the farm, and we spent our two weeks filming them. We saw how the food was distributed, how the animals are cared for. A baby turtle with a cold is given nose-drops. In short, we tried to learn as much as we could about this spectacular undertaking. When we realized that, for an equivalent weight, beef gives 19% protein, chicken 21%, and turtle meat 24%, we understood why the proprietors had such high hopes for their project.

Two tons of equipment, a team of four Indians, two researchers, and us, in French Guiana. This was our second expedition to that area to film the egg-laying of the luth turtles.

A race for life

Of all the spectacles of nature, that of birth is undoubtedly the most beautiful, regardless of whether it is a baby zebra emerging wet from its mother, a pride of lion cubs being licked by a lioness, fishes hatching from their eggs, an infant ostrich stumbling out into the world, a tiny orangutan sliding down between his mother's legs and crying like a baby, or a group of newborn sharks emerging from their mother's stomach and darting off with their mouths open. But I think the most striking means of arrival on earth, so to speak, is that of the turtle.

As the eggs are laid, they fall into the hole in the sand that the mother has dug. The mother then fills the hole. If the turtle is a land turtle, the mother packs down the soil to harden it and keep predators from stealing the eggs. The sea turtle, however, leaves her eggs as soon as she has covered them. About sixty days later, the heat of the sun on the sand makes the eggs hatch. Although the female will return to the same spot to lay her eggs in future years,* she will never make the least effort to care for her offspring.

---

*Dr. Carr tagged 219 turtles. Of that number, 62 returned after two years, and 10% after three years.

Crossing the marshes during our first expedition. The incredible stench almost made us forget about the swarms of mosquitoes. After we left the marsh, our two tons of equipment had to be carried by porters.

The baby turtles, once their eggs hatch in the nest, will be attracted instinctively toward the light and warmth and will climb to the surface of the sand. At that point begins a fantastic race for life. Since the mother turtles lay their eggs at the highest point reached by the tide, the newborn turtles will have a distance of between 100 and 450 feet to cross before reaching the sea.

For the baby turtles, this crossing over a short stretch of sand is like climbing the Himalayas. A small rise in the sand requires an effort almost beyond their strength. In order to find their way, they sometimes follow the smell of the sea spray, but most of the time they are attracted to the luminescence of the shoreline. This indicates that most turtle eggs must hatch at night, following the general law of nature. At night, there are comparatively few natural enemies: a few crabs, wild dogs, sometimes a peccary or a jaguar will kill and eat a certain number of the baby turtles.

But it sometimes happens that the turtles hatch at dawn, just before the sun rises. For these babies, the race to the sea means almost certain death. During the daylight hours, the enemy strikes from above. The frigate birds, circling restlessly overhead, fall like stones to the beach, one after another, seizing this easy prey in their long, hooked beaks. Other frigates arrive, and soon there are almost no turtles left. No more than ten percent of them reach the water. Most of those are caught on the surface by birds or under the water by schools of barracuda, tuna, and ravenous young sharks.

On the Mana River, in French Guiana, after the second day of rain. Indian pilots travel close to shore in order to take advantage of the countercurrent. Below is the first luth turtle we photographed during our second expedition. We took the picture at 11 P.M., at high tide. This specimen was over eight feet in length and weighed about seven hundred pounds.

Hunting for scenes to film can occasionally be a dangerous sport. Here, on the coast of French Guiana, the turtle is harmless but the surf, with its floating tree trunks, can break your legs if you're not careful. The belt I'm carrying on my shoulder in this picture holds the camera's batteries. One secondary advantage of expeditions like this one is that it provides the opportunity to test equipment under the worst conditions.

We filmed this drama of nature at Tromelin Island in the Indian Ocean. The success of the film on television was astonishing, and we received hundreds and hundreds of letters. However, we must remember that the baby turtles do not often hatch during the daylight hours, and that the massacre of newborn turtles by frigate birds is much less frequent than is generally believed.

Hope in Malaysia

"Hello, Chris! Welcome to the land of giant turtles!"

With these words of our friend Ken Skriven, a new adventure was beginning for us. Ken is an ornithologist as well as a travel agent. His specialty is the jungle—the deep jungle. It was also the beginning of long expeditions facilitated by Ken's extraordinary familiarity with the

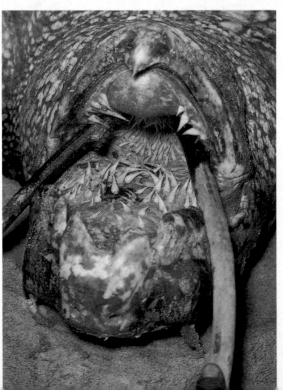

Opposite, upper: Note the baby turtle, the size of a box of matches, on the head of this giant turtle. The newborn turtle will take between seven and ten years to reach a weight of one-half ton.
Opposite, lower: It sometimes happens that eggs are deformed. In such cases, no turtle will hatch, even though the eggs may be fertile. The turtle uses these flexible, horny teeth to chew its food.

Above: Poachers, interrupted in their work by our arrival, did not have time to cut up this turtle. After taking this picture, we wet down the turtle with seawater and pushed her back into the ocean.

language, the people, the animals, and the terrain that we would encounter.

While we were driving toward the east coast in Ken's white Landrover, he told me about the luth turtles of Malaysia. "It's probably the largest concentration of these animals in the world. They come to lay their eggs over a stretch of twenty miles of straight beach, in certain spots. No one knows why. The fishermen here have always known about the luth turtles. In the old days, gathering the eggs was pure chaos. Anybody could take as many eggs as he wanted from any spot on the beach. But, in the last few years, the head of the Department of Fish at Trengganu has established some controls. Eggs can now be taken only in certain areas. Only a certain number of eggs are allowed to be sold in the local markets. And the turtles themselves, of course, are all protected.

"The government, in order to keep the supply of turtles from being depleted, buys a certain number of eggs and re-buries them in the sand, in a hatching ground which is entirely surrounded by a fence. The eggs are placed in holes dug by the keepers, and then covered. The holes are marked with a tag showing the date and place where the eggs were picked up. Then, as further protection, each hole is also enclosed within a fence. When they hatch, the baby turtles are picked up in nets before being set free. The keepers have explicit instructions, however, to let the turtles run over the sand before they are put into the water, so that the babies will have an indelible memory of the place where they were born.

"Every season, there are about a thousand nests; and sixty to seventy percent of the eggs eventually hatch. On the basis of those figures, we feel pretty confident that we're succeeding in saving the species."

It was July, the beginning of the hatching season. Five keepers were in charge of the nursery. There was a stout fence around a stretch of beach 300 yards long and fifty yards wide. Inside the fence, I saw rows of tags, like the labels used in plant nurseries—hundreds and hundreds of them, each one marking the location of a nest. Within the individual enclosures of some of the nests, I could see baby turtles already moving around. The first ones born seemed to emerge from the sand in groups, as though pushed out gently by a slow, regular heartbeat.

Lying in the sand, we filmed the scene. As soon as our lights were turned on, the little turtles started moving toward them. When we shut off the lights, the turtles gradually began turning toward the water. They were counted and then, well before dawn, they were turned loose.

In this way, every night of the hatching season, hundreds of young luth turtles are set free at Trengganu to make their way to the sea. This practice represents one more element of hope for the survival of this species. Malaysian fishermen tell the story of a shipwrecked sailor

Opposite: This photograph, taken in Malaysia, is an image of hope. These baby turtles, having been saved from poachers, have reached the water. At this moment, an ineradicable image of this spot is imprinted on their brains—which are no larger than a grain of rice. The beach at Kuala Terengganu, shown here, is the first luth turtle preserve in the world.

many years ago who was saved and carried to shore on the back of a luth turtle. Perhaps we are beginning to repay his debt.

The lost camera

Since Nadine and I are usually the only ones on our expeditions who know anything about films and photography, we are constantly busy and have little time to keep track of what others are doing. Usually, just before we leave camp, I point with my flashlight to this or that piece of equipment and tell this or that bearer to take it. Nothing is heavy, and nothing is fragile. And we try to carry nothing that can be hurt by the salt air or by the sand. Before we leave I check to see that we have everything we want. Then we set out, Nadine and I and our three bearers, each of us with a flashlight, into the darkness.

On this particular occasion, I was going a distance of only a couple of miles in order to film a mother turtle laying her eggs. The turtle was easy to identify because she was missing one of her hind paws, probably the result of an attack by a shark. We reached the spot, pitched our tent, sorted out our equipment on the beach, and spread out to wait for the turtle. I could see everyone's position because of his or her flashlight.

Finally, the turtle arrived, made her way up the beach, dug her hole, and laid her eggs. Despite her handicap, she seemed to have little difficulty in burying the eggs in the sand.

I looked up at the sky. The stars had disappeared. I could see a squall out over the water, moving toward us. "Quick!" I shouted. "Get everything together! Let's get to the tent!"

We were hardly inside the tent when the squall hit. The raindrops were as big as pigeon eggs.

Nadine busied herself by checking the equipment. "Where's camera number two?" she asked.

"One of the bearers has it. The one who looks like a Roman emperor."

Caesar, knowing that we were talking about him, held out his empty hands to show that he did not have the camera.

"Good Lord!" Nadine exclaimed. "Where's the camera?"

Caesar, with truly imperial dignity, glared at me briefly before pointing slowly toward the beach. "Camera on tree trunk. I get."

There was not a minute to lose, and we all took our flashlights and set out, running across the sand. It was still raining, and our footprints in the crust of the wet sand looked like those of the Abominable Snowman.

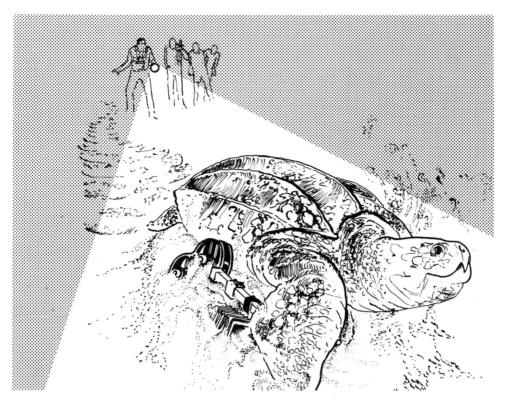

A stroke of luck made it possible for us to find our spare camera under a giant turtle. After a thorough cleaning, it was still working, and we used it throughout the rest of the expedition.

Twice, the beam of my flashlight struck dark, shiny, rocklike objects on the beach: luth turtles laying their eggs. I had to resist the temptation to stop and watch, once more, the miracle of life. There was something more immediately pressing: our work tool, our indispensable means of communicating what we saw, our third eye. . . . If we didn't find it within a few minutes, the rain would almost certainly ruin the wiring of the camera's motor.

"Come on! Hurry!" I yelled.

Caesar, feeling terribly guilty, was more upset than any of us. He was trying desperately to remember which tree trunk it was that he had set the camera down on. On the ocean side of the beach, of course,

Double page following: It is late—almost daylight, and this turtle is still on the beach. Turtles who lay at high tide sometimes have finished laying by the end of the night. Even the most exhausted turtles—like this one—always reach the water before the sun can dry them out and kill them on the beach.

there were no points of reference; on the jungle side, especially in the darkness and rain, everything tended to blend into a single dark mass. To make things easier, we formed a single rank perpendicular to the water and began walking down the beach.

"Christian!" Nadine called. "Over here!"

We rushed to the spot. I got there at the head of a group of four converging flashlights. We looked down, following the beam of Nadine's light. In the center of the group, her shell perpendicular to the trunk of a fallen tree, there was an enormous turtle. She had just finished laying and was covering the eggs, throwing great waves of sand into the hole with her forepaws.

"For God's sake, Nadine! We don't have time for this! We've got to find that camera!"

Nadine, wet to the bone, her hair plastered over her face, did not even turn. "Your camera's right there," she said quietly. "Caesar put it on the trunk, and the turtle must have knocked it over while she was laying her eggs. Anyhow, it's right there, getting buried with her eggs."

I dropped to my knees. I couldn't believe it. My camera, being buried by a turtle. Holding my flashlight in my mouth, I began digging frantically. I forgot how tired I was. I forgot the rain. I even forgot the torrent of sand that the turtle was shovelling at us. "Come on! Everybody dig," I ordered. "Make a circle around the hole."

We must have looked like idiots kneeling there in the rain, digging like madmen, while the turtle, ignoring us completely, continued to shovel in sand as fast as we could scoop it out. I could not help thinking of something that Christo, a friend of mine, had once told me: "The world is divided into creators and imitators."* We were, no doubt, imitators.

Nadine's laugh eased the tension. Then, fortunately for his own peace of mind, Caesar found the camera about a foot below the surface. It was full of sand, but it was not too wet. We heaved a collective sigh of relief. This was followed by a truly gigantic sigh from the turtle. No doubt she was even more relieved than we were.

We returned to the tent and I spent the rest of the night cleaning the camera until the last grain of sand had been removed. By then, we no longer had any need for the flashlights. It was dawn.

When we returned to Paris, I had the camera checked by the

---

*Christo, a genial artist, has a whole theory of creativity: "An idea belongs to the person who originates it. Other people, when they make use of that idea, are only imitators. The originator leads; the others follow."

maintenance department at Arriflex, telling the supervisor only that there had been some sand in the motor. A couple of days later the supervisor telephoned me. "I've checked it out myself," he said, "and it's in perfect shape. There's only one thing that I'd like to know: Why on earth did you put sand in the motor?"

5

Animals in the wild

In the mouth of the lion

John Wolhouter pulled on the reins and brought his horse to a halt. The animal, like John himself, was covered with reddish dust. John's dog, panting, quickly scrambled over to the shady side of the horse. They remained there, waiting motionless with John peering out from under his broad-brimmed hat, tiny dots on the Olifants River plain of South Africa. A carpet of sun-scorched grass extended into the distance, broken by rocks rising from the floor of the savannah. The cry of an eagle echoed from the thick border of vegetation which stretched for twenty-five miles along the bank. When the shadow of the trees reached the horseman's feet, he turned, resting his open hand on the horse's back, and scanned the trail along the river that he had followed. Finally, he caught sight of three mounted Africans, followed closely by five dogs. He spurred his horse and continued his slow progress toward the horizon.

John and his men had been hunting for five days and had killed seven mountain zebras—the most difficult to approach of the zebras, and also the most beautiful, with narrow markings and round ears. The last zebra, wounded in the stomach, had led them on a devil of a chase over pebble-covered hills. The men, the horses, and the dogs, all equally exhausted, were now returning to the farm. The following day, John would send his guide back, with three horses and some game bags, to get the skins which, for the moment, they had left rolled with salt and hidden in a cave. They had piled rocks in the cave's entrance to keep wild animals from reaching the skins.

Opposite: The sheer beauty of wild animals is one of the reasons for trying to save them, just as we would try to preserve a work of art. Nadine took this photograph at the bottom of the Ngorongoro Crater.

Suddenly, John's horse threw back its head and shied. Instinctively, the hunter reached for the rifle resting in his saddle holster. He could feel the horse trembling beneath him. There was danger but as yet John saw nothing. Perhaps it was a snake. He had had the horse for several years and was familiar with its reactions. He turned the animal so as to detour around a large, dead acacia tree. Simultaneously, he felt claws tear into his shoulder; the horse, whinnying in pain, collapsed under him. He saw a female lion spring on the dog and break its back.

John was born in Africa and he knew lions. He had seen ambushes like this one a dozen times. He knew that only female lions hunted in this fashion. The male appeared later, and, if there were cubs, they followed the male. John knew all this. But this was the first time that he himself had been the lions' prey.

There were three lions. One had the dog, which died without a sound. The other had sunk her fangs into the horse's neck. And the third had John on the ground, her great jaws clamped shut on his shoulder. The rifle was somewhere under the horse's body.

John was aware that he had only one chance. If he could remain absolutely motionless, he might at least delay the instant in which the lioness would crush his skull.

He played dead. Despite the four spikelike fangs in his shoulder, the putrid stench of the animal, and the blood that he could now feel wetting his shirt, he lay there, soundless, unmoving, waiting for a miracle. The miracle, in this case, was in the animal's instincts. As soon as a lion is in possession of an assured meal, her instincts tell her what to do: get away from the other lions so that she may enjoy her meal in peace.

The lion raised her head without releasing her prey, and John felt one of her paws being withdrawn from his thigh. Then she began dragging him toward a thorny bush fifty feet away where, no doubt, she intended to make her meal. Twice, the lion paused in her efforts to drag the heavy body to the bush. John still did not move. Then the lion stopped again and turned to look at the horse. In doing so, she released John's shoulder. At that moment, John understood that he had a single chance—a very slim one; slim as the blade of the dagger that he stealthily drew from the scabbard on his belt.

Why hadn't he thought of it before? Because he was terror-stricken. Fear makes one forget simple things. When the lion released his shoulder—gently, as though not to bruise so delicate a dish—John had had a second in which to think. Now as the lion felt him move, she growled but it was too late. John plunged the dagger twice into the tawny fur, burying it to the hilt.

John's three African companions would remember all their lives what they saw that day along the Olifants River. As they approached, they saw the horse flailing about on the ground, her throat between the jaws of a young lion. Then they heard a great roar and as they turned, they saw another lion leap high into the air and then fall to the ground bleeding profusely. She lay there twisting and turning in agony.

Despite the barking of the dogs and the near panic of the horses, the Africans managed to lay John crossways behind one of their saddles. Then they took off at a gallop toward the farm.

That evening, five men returned to the scene of the attack. The vultures and the jackals had already finished stripping the meat from what the lions had left of the horse and dog. They recovered the saddle, harness, and rifle. The dead lion had not been touched. Lying on her side, with her paws together, and her eyes closed, she looked as though she were asleep. Thousands of flies and ants swarmed over the dried blood.

That happened on August 12, 1903.

During my first visit to South Africa, I saw the lion's skin, with its two dagger holes, hanging in one of the lodges of Kruger National Park, where John Wolhouter's dagger is also on exhibit. No doubt they are still there today.

The great yellow cats

We were in Kenya again, a country that we know well and where we have many African and European friends. The brilliant blue of the sky, garnished with thick, white clouds, was our assurance of good weather. The Landrover was loaded down with equipment and supplies and we happily left the city to the tourists and headed out on safari.

At the end of the road leading to Amboseli, at the foot of ancient Kilimanjaro, we turned into the jungle. This is where the country of the Masai begins. Recognizing our vehicle, some of the Masai people waved their arms in friendly welcome. A raised arm, an open hand—the universal and no doubt the first greeting among humans.

The Masai of East Africa are an ancient people. Although they are famous as warriors, they were farmers before they took up arms. A Nilotic subgroup, they are the descendants of tribes that, thousands of years ago, were already established in those regions that today are known as Egypt and Ethiopia. Like their ancestors, they are breeders of cattle. They live on their cattle just as the Eskimos live on seals and the Tuareg on camels. For several months of the year, the Masai drink blood taken from their cattle. The children get blood mixed with milk.

The Masai hold lions simultaneously in great scorn and great veneration. They have no fear of these animals except at night. We often

have been awakened in the middle of the night by a great uproar in the *manyattas* (the mud-hut villages of the Masai people). The old women of the tribe, sensing the presence of a lion nearby, were beating oil cans with gourds to give the alarm and to frighten away the animal.

The respect of the Masai for *Simba*, as they call the lion, is reflected in the costumes they wear on feast days. The young Morane (see glossary) warriors, each proudly holding two metal-tipped spears, decorate their heads with a piece of mane taken from a lion killed by a spear. (Contrary to popular belief, the lion is not necessarily killed by a single warrior, but by a group of them.) Today, the government of Kenya, in an effort to control the hunting of lions, has banned this kind of ornament. Nonetheless, during the ceremonies of initiation, they are still used; and they are obviously made from fresh skins. We've made a film of these ceremonies—ceremonies that few Westerners have ever had the opportunity to witness.

Opposite: In Uganda and Tanzania, whole families of lions climb trees to escape the flies, ox-flies, and mosquitoes.

Upper: Morane warriors are required to kill a lion with a spear before they are initiated into manhood. This young man has never had a haircut.

Lower: Our headlights momentarily blinded this female lion. She growled at us—indicating that her cubs were nearby. These animals rarely attack vehicles, but it did happen to us twice in South Africa. On both occasions, they were lions who were accustomed to vehicles, but they attacked because we had inadvertently disturbed them.

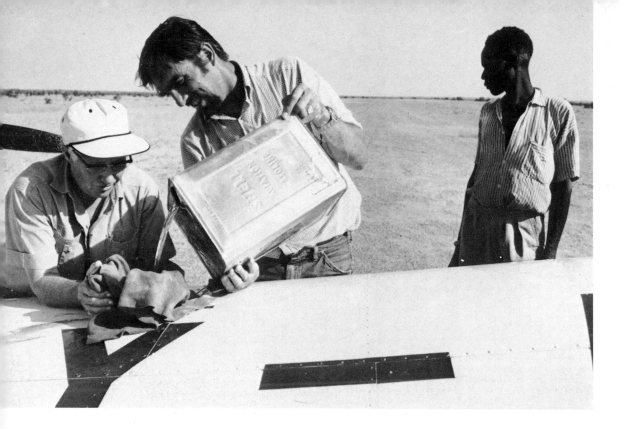

Dr. Spoerry is the flying Schweitzer of Kenya. Without her, we would not have grown to know and love the country as we do. Here, at Lake Rudolf, I am learning the proper way to pour gasoline without spilling any. The trick is to hold the can with the spout upward.

Less than twenty years ago, the Masai were still hunting lions by the methods traditional among their people. A lion was sighted by young shepherds. One of the boys ran back to alert the *manyatta* while the others remained to guard the cattle. The Moranes left immediately for the spot—their spears and shields were always on hand—and they soon had the lion surrounded. With their cowhide shields held before them and their long spears ready, the warriors tightened the circle around the lion. The first spear was cast when the lion attacked. In a few seconds, the lion was lying on the ground, twenty spears in his body.

Sometimes one of the warriors was wounded. If he survived his wounds, the scars were a badge of honor. If he died, daily life in the *manyatta* went on as before.

On three separate occasions, we have witnessed encounters between Masai tribesmen and lions. A warrior, carrying his spears and wearing a length of cloth thrown over his shoulder, strides across a plain. His path takes him very close to a group of lions lying in the grass. The Masai does not slow his pace, let alone detour around the lions. It is the lions who, reluctantly, get to their feet and move to allow the warrior to pass.

The missionaries were of much help to us in Africa. Here, among the Masai at the foot of Kilimanjaro, we are making use of the missionaries' linguistic skills to question a group of Masai girls. We always pitched camp outside the *manyattas*, both to show respect for the privacy of the Masai and to preserve our own standards of hygiene.

The life of a lion

A lion's daily routine may be summarized in one word: sleep. Of all the large cats, the lion spends the most time—eighteen hours out of every twenty-four—stretched out in sleep. This behavior is a source of puzzlement and disappointment to tourists whose idea of lions is based on Hollywood jungle pictures.

Certainly it is true that the lion's life is not one long siesta. We've made lion films in Kenya and Tanzania, and it is rare that a sequence does not show a battle, or a chase, or a game of some kind. These spectacular events do occur, but they occur less frequently than is generally believed.

Unlike most felines, lions live in a family group. One rarely sees a lion alone, and, on such occasions, it is not unlikely that the lion's companions are merely hidden from view. A lion family comprises one or more males and many females and young lions. Family groups of thirty have been observed in various countries of Africa. The largest one that I have ever filmed had seventeen lions. In general, lions are very home-loving creatures and tend to remain in the hunting territory that is theirs.

Lions are polygamous, and, for this reason, are sometimes involved in violent battles. We heard one such encounter at night which lasted more than two hours. The following day, one of the combatants, one eye missing and his nose badly scratched, spent most of his time at the nearby water hole, loss of blood having created an insatiable thirst.

The females, who are often responsible for such battles, are in heat every four or five weeks, year-round. One hundred and five days after the mating, the cubs are born. A litter usually comprises one to six cubs. It will be a year before the young lions are able to shift for themselves. For the first three weeks of their lives, cubs are particularly vulnerable. They are born blind and are not much larger than house cats. Infant mortality is very high. The touching scenes that one sees of cubs romping and playing are only one aspect of jungle life. In reality, things are sometimes very different.

We were in the Ngorongoro Crater in Tanzania one afternoon filming the celebrated black rhinoceroses (whose skins are actually gray), when we caught sight of a group of lions devouring a zebra carcass in the tall grass along the river. We slowed down our Landrover and, cameras at the ready, detoured so as to approach the group. There were two females and five young lions gnawing on the zebra's hindquarters. Less than a hundred yards away, a large, black-maned male was watching. Only his head protruded above the tall grass, but that was sufficient to allow him to keep watch over the females and the cubs.

I shot some photographs of the cubs playing with the zebra's stomach. Then I noticed that one of the cubs was making constant trips between the carcass and a clump of grass not far away. The base of the clump was invisible from where we were, so we moved until we could see it. Behind the grass there was a dead cub, its stomach torn open—no doubt by claws—perhaps by those of the father lion, who continued to stare at us as we moved away.

Possibly the death of the cub was the result of a lesson in manners. Young lions are expected to wait their turn to eat. To violate that elementary law sometimes costs a young lion its life. Among other species—elephants, for example—an unruly youngster is accepted goodnaturedly, just as a mischievous child would be by humans. Lions, however, are not so understanding.

Not all lions are so brutal in dealing with their offspring as the one we saw that day. Throughout the year, in the Nairobi National Preserve, one sees females nursing their young. For that matter, a careful

Opposite: It happens very seldom that a man can approach a lion eating its prey—especially when the man is unarmed and on foot. But it is possible. In fact, it was done, and recorded on film, on two occasions.

Above: Yawning is as catching among lions as it is among people.

Opposite, upper: Mating lasts only a few seconds, but it takes place from sixteen to twenty times a day over a period of as much as four days. Several males participate.

Opposite, lower: These cubs spend their time nursing, playing, and sleeping. The mortality rate among young lions is very high—sometimes as much as 50% or higher for a single litter.

observation of the way lions live will often produce surprising results. Cubs, for instance, will visit a neighboring litter in order to play. If they are there at mealtime, they will not hesitate to share the mother lion's teats with her own brood. These temporary "exchanges" of cubs are common among lions. They have not been observed among other felines, but then, the lion is the only cat that lives in a family.

When food is scarce, young lions are the first to suffer. Since they are not yet able to hunt for themselves, they can feed only on what the older lions leave. Since they are growing and need meat, cubs that have already been weaned are the first to starve. In some years, the mortality rate of young lions reaches fifty-five percent.

Biological equilibrium is often subject to laws that are apparently contradictory and even antinatural. With the help of observers who live in the area, we have been able to capture on film the fragile balance which, in the above case, seems to militate against life.

A wild animal knows nothing that he has not learned from adults. Instinct is often less important than acquired knowledge. This is why it is impossible to set free animals born in captivity.

The southwestern part of Africa consists largely of vast stretches of semidesert areas. The seasons, though discernible, are sometimes irregular. When rain is abundant, the grass reaches its greatest height, and the end of the rainy season is when many species of animal bear their young. In wet years, there is a marked increase in the number of young herbivores. The antelope, zebras, gnu, and gazelles multiply greatly. Then, several months later, the lion cubs are born. It is particu-

Lion cubs, like their parents, sharpen their claws on tree trunks every day. Tigers often use the same trunk for years; but lions are less territorial than tigers and sharpen their claws on any convenient trunk.

larly interesting that the lions' litters are larger than the herbivores' and the lions must kill more antelope, gnu, or zebras to feed their young. The result is that the number of grass eaters is reduced; for an exceptionally rainy year is not followed necessarily by a season favorable to growth of vegetation. In that sense, the lions are regulators of nature's equilibrium. Their presence is necessary in a system in which plants and animals must be constantly in balance.

Once they have finished eating, lions find a place in the shade and take a long nap. Animals who are the lion's natural prey are no longer afraid of the lion once the latter has eaten—even when they see a lion in an open field. (The above photograph was taken with a telescopic lens, in Mozambique.)

The lions of Kruger National Park

There are moments in a journalist's life that he does not easily forget: his first camera, his first article, the first time he saw one of his photographs in a magazine.

One such moment in my life occurred in a New York skyscraper, after a uniformed attendant had directed me to the offices of *Life* magazine. *Life*'s heart beats no longer, but mine was beating wildly when I arrived to try to sell the editors my first photograph of lions. I was not terribly confident. My competitors, I knew, were famous reporters with the best cameras and equipment and the biggest expense accounts. And I was only a greenhorn. I halfway expected to be handed the usual bromide: "Leave us your name and address, and we'll be in touch with you." With the other half of my mind, I could imagine how I would feel when I received an advance copy of some future issue and opened it to the pages containing my photographs.

Subsequently, *Life* published other photographs of mine—porcupines, tigers, elephants—but I shall always have a soft spot in my heart for the magazine because they bought my photographs of lions.

And then, in my photographer's life, there are the "pictures that I'd like to have taken." Among those, in my case, are photographs of the lions of Kruger National Park.

A pride of those felines had taken as their hunting territory an area near a river and intersected by a trail. For years, tourists visited that area in vehicles, both to see the countryside and to observe the animals. Since the trail was quite narrow, most of these vehicles, after leaving the local lodge, headed for a turn in the river and followed the bank to a hippopotamus pool.

While we were making the film *Grand Safari*, Pierre Loustau and I went out one day to get some background footage.* Pierre was driving our Peugeot 404, and I was manning the camera.

We knew that the lions in the area usually waited for antelope to appear alongside the river. But no one had explained to us how this was done.

---

*Theoretically, this footage is used to fill in film sequences. In practice, it is rarely used and remains locked in its can until someone decides to throw it away.

Opposite: Contrary to what many people think, the female lion, and not the male, is the one who hunts. Groups of females often use complex strategy in bringing down their prey. On this occasion, three females were on a plain where a herd of gnu were grazing. Lions 1 and 2, as shown in the sketch on the opposite page, took up positions about forty yards apart. As soon as lion 3 began making a detour around some rocks, the other two flattened themselves against the ground. The gnu, panicked by the scent of lions ahead of them (from lions 1 and 2), turned and tried to run in the opposite direction. At that moment, lion 3 leaped out of her hiding place and, in a single bound, brought down a young female gnu. She was then joined by the other two lions.

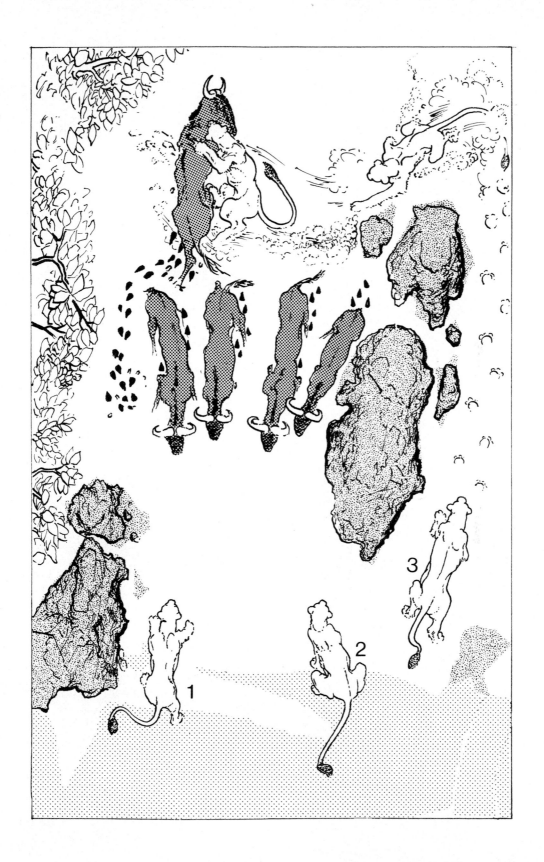

There was a tourist caravan ahead of us on the trail, composed of a half dozen automobiles. Bringing up the end of the line was a large American vehicle. To our left there was a slight slope, bare of all vegetation because of the constant passage of animals on their way to drink. The slope led down to the water, which was muddy because of heavy rain the preceding night. To our right was a growth of underbrush, thinned by the trails beaten by animals making for the river.

The American car ahead of us slowed almost to a halt. We did the same. Between the line of vehicles and the river was a herd of antelope. They seemed to hesitate to drink. From where we were, we could hear the snorting of the melee—a warning that there was danger nearby.

"Maybe there's a crocodile down there," Pierre whispered. "Get your camera ready."

We moved forward about ten feet, then the line of vehicles stopped again. The people ahead of us seemed to be watching the herd. Through the oval-shaped rear window, we could see them waving their hands and pointing toward the antelope. The occupants of the other vehicles shared their excitement. We could hear children exclaiming in delight

These zebras seem fascinated by the sudden death of one of their herd. It goes without saying that it is the sight of the lion, rather than the spectacle of death, that surprises them.

over the antelope. And we could see cameras being raised to photograph the spectacle through the open windows of the vehicles.

Pierre has had much experience both with wild animals and with documentary films. I felt his hand on my arm. "Look at that," he said softly. "To the right."

I looked and could not repress a start. Right next to us, so close that she was almost touching the fender of our vehicle, a female lion had appeared out of nowhere. She did not even seem to be aware of us; her attention was given exclusively to the herd of antelope.

By rising and craning my neck, I could see her perfectly. Her head was low, her neck stretched, and her shoulder blades were tense under the sleek hide.

"Oh, God," I groaned. "There's no way that I can get a picture of that."

Pierre cautiously touched the accelerator with the tip of his toe, and our Peugeot crept forward. The lion, pressed against the vehicle which served to hide her from her prey, moved forward with us. We stopped. She stopped. We moved forward a few feet; so did she. It was as though the lion and the Peugeot had the same engine. We played this little game a while longer, until we were almost touching the rear bumper of the American vehicle ahead of us. No one in the caravan was aware of the lion, and everybody was absorbed in the antelope, watching as three of the animals now lowered their heads and began drinking from the river.

What happened next took no more than a split second. The lion, leaving our fender, crept rapidly to the right-hand side of the vehicle ahead of us. As she moved, she was watching the antelope from under the car. Then she gathered together her paws, her body tensed, and, in a single leap, sprang over the rear end of the vehicle in front to land fifteen or twenty feet from the antelope. The herd panicked and tried to run, but it was too late. In two more leaps, the lion was among them. When the cloud of dust settled, we saw her standing over a dying antelope.

Oh, to be able to have gotten a shot of that prodigious leap over the American car! Unfortunately, my film opened with a lovely shot of the cloud of dust.

The lion's behavior on this occasion is not hard to explain. Hundreds of tourists visit Kruger National Park every day. Several generations of lions have been familiar with automobiles since birth. They are aware that, despite the smell of gasoline (which they do not seem to mind), these vehicles provide a hiding place from which to creep up on their prey. They have not been using that method for very long. Certainly, the generation preceding ours would not have been able to witness this "impact of modern life" on the way lions hunt.

ANIMALS IN THE WILD 205

One may wonder why the antelope did not understand what the lion was doing. Obviously, those who experienced the results of the strategm are no longer alive to explain it to the others. But that is another story.

The tree-dwellers

The first time that *Paris-Match* published our color photographs of a lion in a tree, hundreds of readers wrote outraged letters, accusing the magazine of perpetrating a hoax. Many people apparently believe that, while panthers may very well climb trees, lions are incapable of imitating their spotted cousins.

There are two places where it is particularly easy to see lions of all ages sitting up among the branches of trees, sometimes several yards above the ground: Lake Manyara National Park in Tanzania, and Kigezi, in the western part of Uganda.

We remained in the field for several weeks to study this rather unexpected kind of behavior among lions. The conclusion that we drew—and it is only our own opinion—is that lions climb trees in order to escape from flies, and particularly from the ox-fly. We saw two lions at Lake Manyara who, after eating, climbed up a tree and remained there for five hours and ten minutes.

There are swarms of flies within six feet of the ground, but there are very few of them at twelve feet above the ground. I should point out that I am speaking only of the flies at Lake Manyara. In India, we were sitting in a tree some fifteen feet above the ground waiting for a tiger, and the ox-flies were so numerous that we had to swathe ourselves in mosquito netting in order to be able to work our cameras. If the flies at Lake Manyara and Kigezi stay close to the ground, perhaps the flies elsewhere in Africa do the same thing. If so, why don't the lions elsewhere climb up beyond their reach? No one has yet come up with an explanation.

At Lake Manyara, whole families of lions climb the acacia trees. We've counted five animals in the same tree. Lions will go back to the same tree for several months, though not necessarily to the same branch. The more leaves a tree has, the more desirable most male lions find it. Female lions seem to prefer the fragile acadia trees. We've filmed two of the latter dozing on branches that no human being could possibly have climbed without falling.

Spinage, a specialist and observer in Uganda, has seen a lion twenty feet above the ground in a fig tree. And Spinage's guide, an African, used to walk up to lions, barefooted and without a weapon, to see them run across the savannah and climb the nearest tree. The same

Camouflage is one of the blessings that nature has conferred on the lion. Adults as well as cubs choose dry areas in which to sleep and to hunt. In the latter case, their coats blend in with the dry grass and they are less visible to their prey.

guide, however, would never walk beneath a tree where lions were sitting or napping, for fear that the animals would leap down on him.

While we were shooting our film on elephants at Lake Manyara, on several occasions we saw a lion stretched out on the branch of an acacia tree, looking around at the countryside. An elephant happened by the tree. The lion ignored it, and the elephant ambled slowly under the tree and continued on his way.

Lions in India

Few people are aware that there are lions in India. I should almost say that there *were* lions in India, for Indian lions are on the long list of endangered animals.

I seem to be repeating myself. I'm always mentioning "extinct animals," "endangered species," and "endangered nature."

Children, when discovering the world of animals, create for themselves almost unlimited images of them. They picture a world teeming with millions of birds, millions of mammals, millions of reptiles. A world alive with an almost infinite number of animals. But what, one wonders, will remain of that world in less than one generation? What will the human population explosion leave of our planet? For it is because of humans that the lions of India are on the road to extinction. They are now rarer than the last single-horned rhinoceroses and rarer than the last tigers.

From a distance, the Indian lion is not very different from the African lion. But, on closer inspection, we notice the thicker fur, the tufted tail, and the body slightly smaller than that of the African lion. The largest recorded Indian lion measured eight feet, four inches in length; the largest African lion, ten feet, eight inches.

Indian lions adapt fairly well to captivity. In 1973, there were twenty-one males and twenty-seven females in fourteen zoos throughout the world. They also reproduce in captivity. However, the cubs, like other felines born in zoos, are no longer "wild," and they cannot be turned loose in the jungle to fend for themselves.

The mane of Asian lions is always very full. But the Indian lion is not as impressive as his cousin, the magnificent black-maned Atlas lion (who no longer exists, unfortunately, except in captivity). Formerly, this "king of beasts" ranged over vast territories from Asia Minor to southern Arabia, from Persia to India. This predator, which kept many species of herbivores from multiplying unduly, lived in small groups, hidden in the bush. It is said that he was more indifferent to the presence of man than his African cousin.

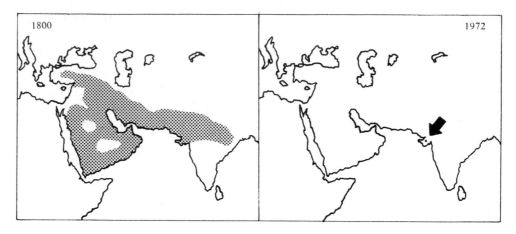

The map on the right shows the habitat of the Indian lion at the beginning of the last century. The one on the right shows it a few years ago. We may see, in the years to come, thousands of other species reduced to tiny points on a map.

It is possible that, at some time, a tiger once met a lion. Some writers and moviemakers have imagined the battle that raged, leaving one of the fighters dead on the ground: the lion. This kind of imagined encounter, it seems to me, is harmful. It creates a false impression of animals and serves only to widen the gap between man and nature. It also shows a total lack of knowledge of animals. Battles between animals of the same species when they meet, be it in the jungle, the ocean, or elsewhere, are infrequent. Between animals of different species, they are even rarer. Obviously, we are talking about such battles as they are presented in certain films, and not about one animal hunting down another in order to eat or about the way in which predatory animals obtain their food. In India, as elsewhere, the large cats avoid one another. Even before they catch sight of one another, they will detour so as to avoid a meeting. Moreover, the lion and the tiger do not occupy the same biotope (see glossary). Finally, we may add that, if a female tiger and a female lion should meet, the lion would not necessarily be at a disadvantage.

The disappearance of the Indian lion, like that of its cousin on the Dark Continent, began with the colonial era and the introduction of firearms. Lions, like tigers, were hunted everywhere, chiefly by two methods, neither of which involved any danger to the hunter. In the first method, an ambush, baited with a calf having a bell around its neck, was set; and the hunter was ensconced safely on a platform high up in a tree. The second method was even simpler and safer: the hunter drove around in a vehicle with a spotlight on the roof. When a lion was spotted, the light blinded it momentarily and it stood there, rooted to the spot, until the hunter shot it. One British officer, a great "sportsman," boasted of having killed 322 lions by the latter method. Another, an officer in a cavalry regiment, claimed "120 lions, lionesses, and lion cubs." At the end of the last century, the Duke of Clarence, brother of King George V, expressed a wish to hunt lions in India. Since the Indian lion was already rare, it was decided to import lions from Africa so that His Royal Highness would not be disappointed. I do not know whether or not this project was actually carried through, but its very existence is indicative of the mentality that prevailed.

Recent statistics obtained by means of studying tracks near water holes are indicative of what the present-day situation is. In 1950, in the Kathiawar Peninsula alone—the Gir Wildlife Sanctuary—in Gujarat, there were 240 lions. In 1955, 290. In 1961, 250. In 1963, 285. In 1968, 162.

During the 1968 census of lions, officials noted that the villagers in the area seemed to have discovered an inexpensive supply of fresh meat. The Maldharies, as these people are known, were in the habit of hiding in the jungle and following lions hunting for food. When a lion brought down an antelope or a buffalo, the men would run out, beating metal drums and shouting. The lion would run away, and the peasants had only to cut off the best pieces of meat, load them into bags, and carry them back to their village. What was left belonged to the lion. One official computed that two of every five animals brought down by lions were thus eaten by humans. In those circumstances, it is not hard to understand why the census-takers found so many lion cubs dead of hunger at Gir.

At the present time, despite an epidemic of hunting by poison in India, the last lions are a protected species. But it is by no means certain that any of our descendants will be able to see an Indian lion living in freedom in the jungle.

With the red men

Nadine, her eyes glued to the road, steered the Landrover as though she were at the helm of a ship. For the past hour, we had been on the road to Uganda, a road as straight as a railway track. We drove as fast as we dared, our vehicle so loaded down with equipment, as always at the beginning of an expedition, that the Landrover's suspension system creaked in protest. There was not a living being in sight anywhere. The broad plain was sun-scorched, deserted, broken only by the cloud of dust stirred up by our wheels. Seen from the air, we would have looked like a ship cleaving her wake through a golden sea.

I knew that I could depend entirely on Nadine's reflexes. My only worry, at the moment, was protecting our fragile lenses and cameras.

"Look," I said, "don't you think we're going rather fast?"

"Of course not. Look at the speedometer."

I looked. It stood at zero. "It's not working," I protested. "If you don't mind, I'd like to get our equipment there intact."

"Fine. Except that if I slow down, we'll feel all the bumps. If we go fast, we won't feel them as much.

"Look at the bustard!"

The large bird, its plumage the color of bread crust, was walking through the grass with measured steps, resembling nothing so much as a miniature ostrich. This bird, its eyebrows marked in black, has always fascinated me. In Ethiopia, we had the opportunity to film one of these animals in somewhat extraordinary circumstances. The bustard was walking in tall grass when a bird—a bee eater—fluttered down and landed on the bustard's back, looking like a horseman in a red helmet. The bustard continued walking, not disturbed in the slightest. The bee eater was waiting for insects to rise from the grass as the bustard passed. Then the rider would catch the insects, eat them, and settle down on the bustard's back to wait for the next tidbit. A singular collaboration.

We were on the road for another twenty minutes before meeting the Masai. We saw two vertical black marks alongside the trail and, as we drew nearer, the marks were transformed into half-naked princes carrying spears. We had encountered these Nilotic shepherds before. They had retained the noble bearing of their distant ancestors in Upper Egypt. On their foreheads and cheeks they exhibited the three red dots of their recent initiation into manhood. They were Moranes.

We did not speak their language, nor they ours, but that was not important. There is nowhere in the world that you cannot use signs to invite someone to get into your vehicle. But, since there was not room in our Landrover for a mouse, let alone for two Masai warriors, I invited them to climb up onto the roof. They were delighted. And so was I.

"Nadine," I cautioned. "Don't go too fast."

"Don't worry," she answered. "Didn't you notice how much the younger one looked like Jacky Stewart?"

She burst out laughing, and the two Masai joined in.

Five days later, we were still in their village. This particular *manyatta* was a group of seven huts smeared with cow dung. It had a population of about forty humans, 200 lean cows, three donkeys, and a dozen dogs: a settlement of shepherds rather typical of East Africa. And, like most poor people, the inhabitants of the *manyatta* were extremely hospitable.

Our camp was outside the village beyond the high fence. Every night, after the last calf had entered the enclosure, the gate in the fence

This unusual picture shows the most recent initiation of Masai warriors. The men's bodies are painted with secret vegetable and mineral colors. Note that their headdresses are made of lions' skins and ostrich plumes.

was carefully closed. But every day, the red men—they use vegetable and mineral colors to decorate their bodies—came to chat, sitting on their heels in a way that no white man can hope to imitate. Two young men, who had learned three or four words of English on various safaris, served as our interpreters.

On the third day, we spoke of lions. For the Masai, the lion is not a "sacred" animal. In the Masai view, the lion, like all other animals, is an inhabitant of the savannah. It is dangerous only when it has cubs. Unlike other Africans, who are often terrified of lions, the Masai have no fear of these animals. Hunting lions with spears is no longer allowed, but the last Masai, many of whose children abandon the nomadic life in order to go to school, still hunt lions in secret. The hunt is now more a matter of courage than of necessity, for the number of animals has greatly diminished on the whole of the African continent.

There were twenty males in the village, nine of whom were adults. Of these nine, seven had headdresses made of the hide of lions. It took a great deal of diplomatic maneuvering, as we sat crosslegged on the beaten earth in the midst of a swarm of flies, to persuade the Moranes to show us these ornamental headdresses. So far as we were able to tell by inspecting these pieces of mane, it appeared that at least three lions had been killed during the year by the men of the *manyatta*. This is a very small number compared to the slaughters organized by certain commercial enterprises in central Africa.

Seeing that we were interested in these ornaments, one of the women went into her hut and came out carrying three dried paws from a young lion. It was thanks to Nadine's presence that, after many circumlocutions, I was able to find out what these paws are used for. When a woman is pregnant, her stomach is rubbed with the paws of a lion killed by the men of the village. The strength, courage, and virility of the lion will then pass into the baby's body. If the baby is a boy, it will be stronger than the son of a woman whose stomach has not been rubbed. "Rubbed" may be too gentle a term. One older woman showed Nadine a young wife whose stomach had been scratched by the claws until it bled. We could not understand how that young woman did not die of tetanus.*

The calm and the storm

It is undeniable that lions attempt to lighten the burdens of shepherds by relieving them of their cows and goats. It happens only rarely, however, that humans are killed by lions. Nonetheless, accidents do happen, particularly with tourists. When people who know nothing about lions see these animals stretched out in the grass a few yards away from a vehicle, they forget that that outwardly placid creature is a

---

*Wounds from claws that have been in contact with putrified meat, like wounds from the bites of monkeys, wild animals, and even sea lions, require great care.

wild animal, a carnivore for whom the search for food sometimes follows the path of least resistance.

In some of the East African preserves, camping areas are set aside for tourists traveling on limited budgets. It is suggested to the people using these areas that, at night, they close their tent-flaps tightly. It seems that mosquitoes often prefer the blood of tourists to that of zebras.

Since the sun goes down at 6 P.M., the nights tend to be rather long. For this reason, two young American tourists, after a long day of picture taking, decided to relax by having a few drinks at the bar of the nearby lodge. "They drank as they usually did," one of the guards told me, "just enough so that they could still find their way back to their tent, and just enough to be able to wake up the whole jungle with their singing."

The two young men reached their tent. Their camp beds had been made by the diligent "boys" of the preserve. One of the men simply fell into his bed, fully clothed, and went to sleep immediately. The other, more in control of himself and more aware of the heat of the African night, took the time to make himself comfortable. He undressed and put on a pair of pajama bottoms. Then, in order to take advantage of the breeze, he moved his bed so that he could sleep with his head outside of the tent. Then he lay down and went to sleep.

The next morning, the first man woke up and was surprised to find himself alone in the tent. The other bed was empty. He immediately reported his friend's disappearance to the chief guard. The African saw at once what the tourist had not seen: next to the head of his friend's bed were the deep paw prints of one or more lions.

The bloody pajama pants of the young man were found almost a half-mile away. The tracks on the trail made it possible to find the animals responsible: two young female lions, less than five years old. Apparently one of them had wandered through the camp and had simply clamped her jaws shut around the man's head, crushing his skull. Then she had dragged the corpse into the brush and invited her friend to join her in the feast.

In order to avoid similar tragedies, it was necessary secretly to hunt down several young lions living in the area of the camp—presumably so that human beings could still believe that they alone were king of the animals.

Animals in captivity

"Mama, is he mean?"
The child was standing face to face with a lion, his eyes level with

Opposite: This lion has climbed a tree to take a nap without being bothered by insects.

Above: Lions are placid animals, as this photo taken from a vehicle shows. But the photographer must be on his guard. Lions are very light sleepers; and the sound of a door opening or of a footstep on the grass will bring him to full alert.

the bottom of the cage. He was fascinated by the great, tawny animal lying in the sawdust.

The circus had arrived that morning. Like a dream, it would vanish by the next morning, taking away the menagerie which it advertised, in giant red letters, as "the finest collection of wild animals in the world." I was tempted to write under the sign, "in the smallest cages in the world." There are thousands of animals who spend their whole lives imprisoned in tiny, filthy cages.

The child watched the lion. The animal, bored and listless, was drowsing.

A part-time keeper of the menagerie happened by, carrying a long iron bar in his hand.

"Come on, Tarzan! Attack! Attack!" he shouted, banging the iron bar against the cage and then jabbing the lion twice in the flank.

The ensuing roar made the crowd draw back. The keeper laughed. The child was terrified and clutched at his mother, who led him away by the hand. "There, you can see for yourself," she told the boy. "Lions are mean and nasty!"

I've seen that scene repeated twenty times, and twenty times I've told myself that animals in captivity should be the subject of broadcasts, articles, and books.

Everyone agrees that certain reforms must be made. Everyone agrees in applauding that old-fashioned, nostalgic spectacle, the circus—so long as certain things are corrected.

I myself love the circus. Children particularly love it. And when we love something, we look at it, watch it carefully, and observe what it is doing. In observing circuses in Europe and elsewhere, I've been struck by one unacceptable aspect of this fabulous spectacle: the training and living conditions of some of the animals. There is virtually no legislation on this point, and the laws that do exist are rarely enforced.

I've seen many performances and spoken to many animal trainers. I've followed circuses closely enough to know how the animals are treated. (I'm speaking of the lions, panthers, tigers, jaguars, and other wild animals more or less trained and, for a sum, exhibited to the public.) Yet, I have never been allowed—not to say that I have been forbidden—to be present at the training sessions that precede an animal's performance in public. I've never been permitted to see how, beginning with a lion cub born in a cage, a trainer turns an animal into a circus performer.

Lions are not naturally inclined to physical effort. And, since they are fed in captivity without the slightest effort on their part, they will not perform in a circus, or anywhere else, unless they are forced to do so—or unless they have a memory of being forced to do so in the past. A performing animal learns every step of his routine by heart. He even learns when to roar so as to heighten the drama of the spectacle. When there is an accident—a trainer is clawed, or even eaten under the spotlights—it is often the result of a calculated risk on the trainer's part in which pride plays a greater part than prudence. In such instances, the other animals in the cage sit, terrified, not budging from their stools, waiting for the order that will send them scurrying back to their cages.

Real courage in dealing with animals is not that easy to find. Nonetheless, I was able to film one such instance on a December afternoon in Africa. It was the middle of the rainy season. Two female lions had just brought down a giraffe. Almost immediately, three black-maned males appeared on the scene. The females withdrew, growling, to wait patiently under a nearby acacia tree.

A European guard approached in a Landrover. He brought his vehicle to a halt and got out less than twenty yards from the carcass. He was unarmed and even without gloves. He walked quickly toward the three feeding lions. One of the males looked up, and then, his tail held low, hurried to join the females. The other two allowed the man to come within ten yards before running off in their turn. They sat in a nearby thicket, watching the man and the giraffe. The guard walked around the carcass, took out his knife, and cut off the animal's head. It would be used in studying the skulls of giraffes. He walked calmly back to his vehicle, threw the head into the rear seat, jumped in, and drove off. I wonder if there is a single animal trainer capable of doing the same thing.

Lions in Israel

I jumped into the taxi and held out a piece of paper to the driver. "General Yoffé," I said. "Do you know him?"

"I know him," he replied.

The ancient Dodge moved silently through the suburbs of Tel Aviv. Curly haired children were playing ball. I saw a man in uniform, a machine gun strapped on his back, waiting for a bus.

I had been in the land of Moses for only one hour. Before I left for Israel, friends had advised me: "Go to see General Yoffé as soon as you arrive, and tell him that you're a friend of ours. He's a remarkable man." I had no way of knowing yet that my "star" would once more bring me into contact with a truly extraordinary man.

The taxi was following an army truck. The back of the truck was filled with young women in uniform who were amusing themselves by making uncomplimentary gestures at passersby and then laughing uproariously.

I tried to place the name. Yoffé. Yoffé. As always when I'm in a strange country, names of people and of streets, as well as telephone numbers, elude me completely. But, for some reason, I suddenly remembered Yoffé! One of the heroes of the Six Day War. And I was not particularly fond of military types.

My taxi stopped. I was there.

I entered the building. There were boxes in the hallways. I heard typewriters clacking away and telephones ringing. I was directed to a door. I opened it and entered a sun-drenched office. A large, bronzed hand was extended. Yoffé was wearing a short-sleeved shirt with an open collar. He had the straightforward look that one associates with sportsmen and true leaders.

I was there because General Yoffé is the leader of the nature pro-

Double page following: It is degrading for man to deprive an animal of its freedom, even though the animal may have been born in a cage. This lion's cage is hardly larger than his body. In his eyes, we can read the story of his suffering during the eight years of his captivity.

tection movement in Israel. He had an interesting idea, and it was going to be my job to translate that idea into a television film.

I felt the film taking shape as the general explained his project to me. As in any true story, the action would be simple. Many shots of the countryside. Much poetry. Without even seeing Israel, I knew that it would be both an exciting documentary film and a boost for the cause of conservation. I could not resist it.

Yoffé started with a basic idea. He took a Bible and made a list of the wild animals living in Israel at the time of Christ. His ambition was to have those same animals living in Israel in the twentieth century.

The fact that boundaries, and the land itself, had changed in the last 2,000 years seemed to make little difference to him. The animals were once there. They may have disappeared from Israel, but the same species were in existence elsewhere. They would be reintroduced into several national parks to be chosen by ecologists and by people from the preserves. The fact that the preserves had vast stretches of desert bordering areas covered with vegetation, made it possible for the general to realize his plan. At this moment, a first group of onagers (wild donkeys), cousins of the ancestor of the donkey, are running loose there. Gazelles, many species of birds, and some rare species of reptiles, are also in the preserve. Yet there was still much to do; for the list of animals in Israel in Christ's time is quite long. The problem, at the time I spoke to General Yoffé, was that of finances. I suggested that we make a film explaining the idea and what it would accomplish. Beautiful background music (which is easy to find in Israel); sweeping views of the scenery in the preserve. No animals and no humans. We'd use photographs to show the species inhabiting Israel in biblical times. And there would be figures at the bottom of each photo: Three ostriches, $1,000. A herd of zebras, $3,000. Bustards, $500. Oryx, $4,000. Two lions, $2,500.

In order to raise money for the preserve, General Yoffé and I would show the film in countries where we had friends. At set times during the showings, after we had already explained the project and showed the still pictures of the animals and the prices, we would turn on the lights in the room.

"All right," we'd say. "Who's for the ostriches? You, madam? Thank you. Someone will come for your check. We thank you for the ostriches! Who's next?"

When the lights would go out, we would show a spectacular panorama of the desert at night, the land of the antelope and the white oryx, followed by a picture (and the price) of these animals. On went the lights, and we began again: "Who wants a white oryx? Four thousand dollars! Thank you, sir. You are the proud godfather of a white oryx.

"And now the lions. They're very cheap: less than thirteen hundred dollars per lion. Who wants it? . . ."

Lions in Israel—free, useful, and happy.

Two years later, the Yom Kippur War broke out just as we were getting to work. We did not cancel our plans, but only delayed them. I know in my heart that, in the near future, men from all over the world will go to Israel on camera safaris. Children, their noses pressed against the window of a Landrover, will ask their parents: "Daddy, did Jesus really see lions?"

The last minute

Chance sometimes plays strange tricks. Just as I was writing the lines above, my telephone rang. I answered:

"Hello? Mr. Zuber? You don't know me, but I know you from television. I've been meaning to call you. Look, I'm a former animal trainer. I'm now retired. I love animals, and that's why I want to talk to you. It's really a scandal how animals are being treated. I don't want to tell you about it now because you won't believe me. What I'd like to do is take you to see how animals are tortured to train them to perform in circuses. Maybe you'd like to make a film of it. You can't imagine what it's like!

"I'm not doing this for money. I believe that you're sincere in what you're doing, and I'm disgusted by what people are doing to animals today. If you have a strong stomach, I'd like to show you what I mean. . . ."

I wonder whether this telephone call is really going to let me find out the truth about the hell behind the glitter of the Big Top. Is my caller motivated by some kind of resentment or jealousy? Or by money, as in the case of the baby seals? Will I discover a scandal that everybody wants to cover up? At this moment, I have no way of knowing. All I know is that it is an exciting life, especially when one is armed with a camera!

The exploration of Africa sometimes has unusual twists. The menfolk of a Sudan village refused to become our bearers, regardless of what we were willing to pay them. Thereupon, their wives took the job.

6

Animals in danger

Television: nature's savior

No one had spoken for the past several minutes. The field rose to meet us and the airplane leveled off. We felt the landing gear make contact with the ground, and we shot past the landing lights before turning at the end of the strip. Suddenly, we seemed hardly to be moving as we taxied toward the terminal buildings at Le Bourget.

I had just completed my fifth round-the-world tour. In one of my aluminum boxes, I had eighteen cans of color film: the result of visits to the shops of traders in animals and animal hides which I had discovered on the basis of a few hints, much patience and, I must admit, sometimes incredible luck. We had been able to remove the mystery from the black market in alligator hides, from the traffic in tiger skins, from the poaching of panthers, the massacre of iguanas, and the illegal trade in ivory. There was the matter of trading in hundreds of thousands of birds: the thousands of birds that were killed so as to be stuffed and sold to tourists; the commerce in lumber and the authorized destruction of forests and jungles; the importing and exporting of wild animals. All the aspects of the shocking exploitation of nature of which we speak all too rarely.

We have been able to lay all our cards openly on the table as far as these problems are concerned. We are free agents. We do not own zoos, or preserves, or aquariums. We do not trade in wild animals. We have no forests to exploit. We do not have to make decisions on matters of hunting and fishing. We do not have to make an accounting to any government, and we have no commercial ties with any factory polluting the environment. We are free. Our only commitment is to our camera: to our photographs and our films. No panther has ever died from being photographed, even if he is the subject of a hundred pictures; but thousands of panthers have disappeared by being hunted a single time.

Everywhere in the world, the territory of the creatures with whom

I am holding about five thousand dollars in my hands. Rhinoceros horns are still greatly in demand.

we share the earth—the animals and plants—is shrinking under the impact of the human population explosion. Soon, we will be at the point of no return.

I had a close-combat instructor in the army who used to give an excellent bit of advice: "Use your mind first." In dealing with this problem as with all others, we must first use our minds. And common sense tells us that we must make use of the most effective means of informing people of the situation. In this sense, I earnestly believe that television will be the salvation of nature.

Occupational hazards

Going after pictures and films is fun—but only if you succeed in getting the pictures and films. And, as in doing anything that is worthwhile, there are risks that must be taken. The cameraman or the photographer, unlike the hunter, has no rifle to bring down an attacking animal. He has only his little black box. Even if he feels perfectly safe at the moment that he's shooting his pictures—as all great journalists say they do—what happens when you've finished the pictures is not always what you'd like.

Nadine and I were once on an expedition in the south of Ethiopia, along with our friends Yves and Françoise Coppens, a dozen other Europeans, and thirty Africans. We were living in huge tents under a blazing sun. Our mission was to try to find relics of our human ancestors—in this instance, human teeth.

Our camp near the Omo River was at the edge of a plateau, in the middle of the bush. The winding river was about two miles away, as the

These two rhinoceroses have just
emerged from their mud bath. They
are in constant danger, night and
day, of being killed for their horns.
Kasiranga, in the north of India, is
the last and most magnificent sanctuary of these animals.

The Mountain tapir is disappearing
because of the great demand from
zoos and because of the commercial exploitation of wild animals.
This animal, tamed by a missionary,
would inevitably be killed and eaten
by jaguars if he were not locked in a
cage every night.

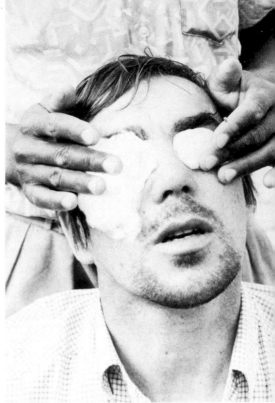

A five-foot cobra can spit its venom a distance of over six feet. I got a spurt of venom in my eyes while shooting this picture, and was blind for three days and three nights. It's not an experience that I want to share with other cameramen.

crow flies. The rest of the region was parched by the sun and incredibly dusty. It would remain so until the rainy season.

On this particular day, some of the Africans were busy preparing the midday meal. Yves was seated at a large table loaded with fossils, trying to decipher some aspect of man's past. Nadine was checking our precious equipment. And Françoise was in her tent, brushing her teeth.

We heard a scream and I saw Françoise run out of the tent, holding a glass in one hand and her toothbrush in the other. "Hurry!" she shouted. "There's a huge snake in my tent!"

Knowing from experience that a "huge snake" is always a medium-sized snake, and that a "medium-sized snake" is always tiny, I was not in a terrible hurry to rescue Françoise. Nonetheless, when I reached the tent I caught a glimpse of about half the body of a snake of fair size—about five feet long—slithering between the tent and the nearby rocks.

There was no mystery about the snake's presence in our camp. A few days before, a naked shepherd from a neighboring tribe had arrived in our camp after walking twenty-five miles across the desert. He offered to exchange a young hare he was carrying—a frightened creature, with large eyes surrounded by immense lashes—for water and food. Françoise could not resist taking the animal. After the shepherd had drunk five dippers of water and had taken enough food to last for the rest of his trek across the desert, the hare was given quarters in a box in the Coppens' tent, fed with a baby's bottle, and pampered and spoiled to within an inch of its life. Its presence, however, had attracted the snake.

Fortunately, I had time to grab a camera, and I was now standing about five feet away from the snake, clicking away at it.

I do not have a particular fondness for things that crawl, bite, and sometimes kill. But I do know something about snakes, and knowledge sometimes banishes revulsion. I knew that this was a cobra, and I watched as the snake raised the forward part of its body above the ground and spread its hood, following my every movement with its head. I continued to take pictures, drawing closer to the reptile but still remaining outside its attack zone.

Nadine and Françoise were watching. "Christian! Be careful," Nadine ordered.

Further away, the Africans were also watching. They were terrified.

"Get me a bag or something," I called out. "I want to catch it for James."*

Coppens' assistant, an excellent research man, took his courage in both hands and brought me a red plastic bucket. I took the bucket and turned back toward the snake. When I saw the cobra, a fraction of a second later, it had its mouth open. Almost simultaneously, I felt a liquid strike me in the eyes. It was a spitting cobra! At once, I felt a terrible burning sensation in both eyes.

"I can't see!" I shouted. "I'm blind!"

I felt hands on my arms, supporting me. Everything began to spin, and I stumbled backwards. Coppens' assistant caught me. "Don't worry," he said. "It's not serious. Come with me." There was a note of false optimism in his voice that I caught immediately. "The doctor's in the camp. Everything will be all right."

The camp was less than fifty yards away. I stumbled over the stones, holding my hands over my eyes. By then, I could not even open my eyes, and the pain was rapidly becoming unbearable.

"Somebody try to kill the snake," I suggested, "so that we'll know what kind of poison it is."

I could already imagine myself at the hospital. That was absurd, of

---

*James Ash, then director of the Snake Park at Nairobi.

Double page following: These Asian crocodiles will be converted into shoes and purses. They are no luckier than their Latin American cousins, who will be sold to tourists as souvenirs. These animals are skinned alive because "the skin comes off more easily."

course. The nearest hospital was 600 miles away, and we had no airplane. By Landrover, it was a three-day journey.

"My God!" Nadine cried. "Christian! Your eyes!"

"It's nothing," I said. "Try to kill the snake. Get the doctor. And then try to get some photographs."

I felt as though someone had mashed live coals against my eyes.

Someone helped me into a sitting position. Dr. Rodin was there now, and he gently wiped my eyes with cotton pads. I still could not open my lids. And the pain seemed to be getting even worse.

I was furious at myself for having been so careless. It was my first contact with a spitting cobra. This specimen seemed closely related to another species which, rather than spitting its venom, bites its victims. The spitting cobra is able to throw its venom a distance of six feet. It aims at what shines—in this case, my eyes. Spitting is its method of hunting and also of defense.

I was very much afraid. I could feel the sweat running down my spine. Meanwhile, Dr. Rodin, sitting on a box in front of me, was trying to work out a solution. Two damp cotton pads were placed over my eyes. I felt the doctor's hand on my bare shoulder. "Christian," he said gravely. "It's quite bad, and I don't have what I need to treat you. I'll have to call Nairobi on the radio. I want you to lie down. Try to stay calm. And tell me what you feel."

"I can't see anything, and my eyes burn like fire. Isn't there anything you can do?"

"Lie down in your tent. Drink a lot of liquids. I'll stay with you."

In other words, he was telling me that there was nothing he could do. Fear drove away the pain for a moment. I began walking, my head held up, like a blind man.

I felt the heat within the tent. Groping for my bed, I lay down on my back. My eyes were bandaged; it occurred to me that the bandage was like the blindfold of a man condemned to die. I felt Nadine's hand in mine, trembling.

I was so afraid that I began stuttering. "C-c-can you im-m-agine letting m-m-myself g-g-get bitten like a greenhorn? D-did you kill it?"

Yes, the snake had been killed. The assistant did it with a spade, but not before getting a few drops of the snake's venom on his face, but not in his eyes. I had been the privileged one. I had gotten the whole sac of venom, and not a drop on my chin or in my hair. All of it in my eyes.

Medical instructions arrived from Nairobi in less than an hour. Yves Coppens told me the good news. "We're going to take care of you

Opposite: In Brazil, crocodiles are caught with a noose, as shown in the sketch. This method has the advantage of being silent; there are no shots to give away the poacher's location. It is quite dangerous for the poacher, nonetheless.

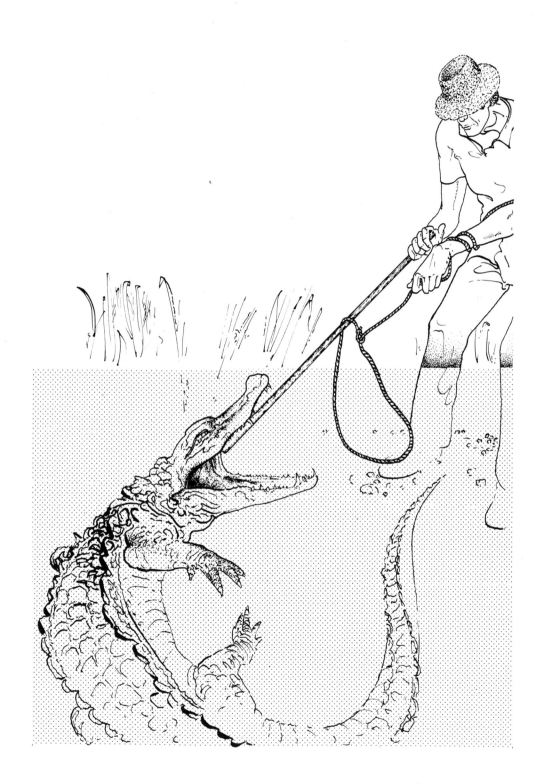

here. We have everything that we need. It'll be all right. Don't worry. If we should need an airplane, we'll get one. You can count on me.''

While waiting, I felt my heart beating in my chest like a drum. It seemed irregular, as though one of the plugs was not firing. It slowed down. Slowed again. Then started up. I was terrified.

I was blind for three days and three nights. It was absolute, total darkness. I tried to forget the pain. But I could not forget the possibility that I might never see again. How could I live without my eyes? I still shiver when I think of it.

I was made to drink quart after quart of tea, and I was to lie as still as possible. This was supposed to help take the strain off my heart. It was enough to nauseate the most avid tea drinker.

A month later, after a check-up by a specialist in Nairobi who assured me that I was doing well and that I was an exceptionally lucky person (the tears of pain, and the initial care that I was given had washed away much of the snake's venom) I went to thank the technicians at the communications center for their help. All communications are by radio-telephone and, in case of emergency, the center assigns priorities to calls. I also visited James Ash, director of the Snake Park.

''You must have a guardian angel watching over you,'' James said. ''When the telephone rang, it was noon on Friday, and I was already at the door on my way out. I had just gotten a boat and I was going to start painting it. I would have been out the whole weekend. I don't know what made me come back to answer the telephone. Habit, I suppose;

Opposite: On Îsles des Saintes in Guadeloupe there were once many iguanas. The tourist invasion has created a market for souvenirs (above and below), and these harmless reptiles are now in imminent danger of extinction.

and a guilty conscience. I had no idea what it was about. But I was able to tell them what to do. Still, you're lucky to be alive. I have two spitting cobras in glass cages here, but I never go to their cages unless I'm wearing a diving mask."

Hell on Îsles des Saintes

A new breed of indirect killers is developing: tourists. The tourist trade, with the buying power that tourists bring, is sharing actively in the disappearance of many species of animals: tiger skins in India; shells in the Bahamas and in Mauritius; Venezuela for stuffed crocodiles; Guiana for flowers and feathers; Kenya for souvenir teeth and horns; and everywhere in India and Africa for ivory.

On three occasions, we've visited beautiful Îles des Saintes in Guadeloupe. Five years ago there were numerous iguanas there. Now, the number is greatly reduced. And each year, as the flow of tourists increases, more and more of these reptiles are killed. Stuffed iguanas, it seems, are greatly favored by tourists as decorative items. One must have seen the elderly American ladies with their blue hair, the angular British women, and the arm-waving Frenchwomen, to realize how successful this item is as a souvenir. We've filmed them buying, buying, buying—without realizing what they were doing.

The last time we were on Îsles des Saintes, we met the local mayor. This elected official pointed out to us, in connection with the problem of protecting the iguanas, that the "poachers," as we called them, were also the island's voters. It was a classic vicious circle, to which I replied as follows: "We're not talking about cutting down on the number of tourists. The fishermen have to live, but so do the iguanas. Why not organize camera safaris? They do it in Africa and India for the rhinoceroses, and the same animal gets sold 200 times rather than just once. All you'd have to do would be to hide the photographers behind blinds in the shrubbery. Make feeding places for the iguanas (if there are any still alive by then) and set up soft-drink stands for the tourists. Inaugurate the camera safaris by inviting some Italian actress to come with her camera. Ban the hunting and capturing and trading in iguanas. And then hope that new generations of these reptiles will forget their fear of men and learn to pose for the tourists."

In fairness, I must add that the mayor accepted this proposal. It must now be put into effect—and appropriate legislation must be enacted before it is too late.

Information is conservation

I am fortunate enough to enjoy what I do for a living. Despite our continual financial problems—we are the only team in France that receives no governmental subsidies—my various undertakings (like this book) make it possible for me to donate two months of my time every year to the World Wildlife Fund.

In the W.W.F. organizational chart at Morges, Switzerland, my name appears on the Publicity and Public Relations Committee. I have the same function in the French section of the Fund.

Within the Fund itself, precious time is sometimes lost in conferences, meetings, and discussions. This, of course, is a necessary evil. No organization can function without a bureaucratic structure of some kind. But I have no doubt that, if I have any value at all to the Fund, it is when I am behind a camera rather than behind a desk.

As much as I dislike office work of any kind, I am nonetheless required to spend some time at the Fund headquarters at Morges between expeditions, if for no other reason than to see the mail. The hundreds of letters we receive after a television broadcast often contain suggestions for future films, case histories of the abuse of nature, and advice: "Why don't you do something for (or against) hunting; the abuse of horses and other domestic animals; the killing of pigeons; horse racing; the commercialization of dolphins and other marine animals used in public shows; baby seals in Canada; pollution of the beaches... slaughter of marine animals; bullfights; vivisection; slaughterhouses; the sale of turtles; the whales; the living conditions of animals in zoos; and so forth.

The overall message I get from this influx of mail is that the public is becoming conscious of the urgency of doing something to protect nature, that people are getting a new image of nature in which dignity plays a part. It also means—and this is one of my chief concerns—that the public wants to know what is going on. People want information. Especially young people. That is one of the principal reasons for our television broadcasts.

It seems to me that the worldwide conservation movement has reached the point where we must begin to make certain elementary distinctions. Let us go back to the question of hunting for a moment. Why is it that, in every country, the very small minority of people who have hunting licenses are able to put such pressure on legislators that the latter are virtually reduced to stasis? And, even more interesting, why is it that the vast majority, who do not care for hunting, are never heard from by these same legislators?

Why do we allow thousands and thousands of homeless dogs and

Commercial traffic in skins and ivory encourages poaching. This photograph of an elephant rifle trap, taken in a preserve in Sri Lanka, shows only one of the methods used by poachers. The purpose of the trap is to wound the elephant.

Opposite: In 1920, the pigmy boar was considered extinct. Then, in 1972, five living specimens were discovered in Assam. It is now one of the rarest mammals in the world.

cats to be born every year, to suffer and die, rather than set up a sterilization program?

Why not establish ways to inform the public of what is happening to animals? Tell people, for instance, about the dolphins who were electrocuted in a pool in one of France's large cities. Tell them about the monkeys that die every week, in some very famous zoos, from lack of proper care. Tell them how the slaughter of seals has begun again; that the hunting of whales is still going on; that hundreds of rivers are becoming increasingly polluted.

In disseminating this information, however, we must be careful also to distinguish the wheat from the chaff. There are hunters who respect game. There are ship owners who are sincerely concerned about oil spills. There are zoos worthy of the name.

It also seems to me, as I've already said, that we absolutely must have, at the international level, a "captivity index." That is, two lists: one of animals capable of surviving comfortably in captivity in certain well-defined conditions; the other, of species that are rare in nature and whose presence in captivity contributes to their disappearance from the wild. Obviously, animals on the second list must be protected from all commercial exploitation, collectors, and public spectacles.

I am convinced that the first zoo to post a sign on its gate saying that, "The animals in this zoo are not in danger of extinction," will draw a huge number of visitors. The exception, of course, must be those cases in which the last living specimens of a species are in captivity. I think that, within the next ten years, this idea will spread. The endangered species no doubt hope that it will, as do their friends.

Human interference

Our proximate ancestors, as opposed to our remote ancestors, were eaters of fruits, vegetables, eggs, and fish. But they also hunted in order to obtain furs. Contrary to the depictions that we usually see of Cro-Magnon man, the Cro-Magnons probably wore their furs inside out; that is, with the fur on the inside, so as to conserve heat. A million years ago, the natural environment was not in danger of disruption. Men killed animals and animals killed men. It is reasonable to suppose that, given the number of animals, the fact that our ancestors hunted had little effect upon the ecological balance.

It is likely that, when the first feline furs were worn by man, they were intended (as they are among the Masai today) as proof of the wearer's courage. The fur was the prize of the victor, a mark of superiority. Even today, the hunting of lions by spear, as it is practiced among certain tribes, has no noticeable impact on the lion population. The Indians along the Amazon—among whom we've lived—since they are unaware of the value of jaguar skins, kill only four or five of these cats every year. Similarly, in Ethiopia, even when the Dassanech or other tribes killed cheetahs who preyed on their flocks, there were cheetahs everywhere. It was not until cheetah furs became valuable that the species was endangered. And this dramatic change took only a few years.

George Budowski, a specialist who is well informed on the question of furs, has this to say: "There have been many abuses of the system of control which consists in stamping the skins in the inventory to be liquidated, so as to distinguish them from new skins. I don't understand how it is possible really to control this operation. Many furriers who try to act properly have been victimized by the lack of honesty of less scrupulous fur traders."

In 1973, an international convention banned traffic in the skins of endangered species. Despite that convention, many furriers have continued to buy skins in violation at least of the spirit of the law.

Here is another viewpoint, that of Guy Mountfort, who specializes in tigers: "The problem has to be considered from the angle of the commercial risk involved. When a furrier buys furs, he is in the same position as a car dealer who buys cars. The next year the models change—and the dealer is 'stuck' with last year's inventory. When fashions change—and we're doing all we can to make sure that they do—the furrier is going to have to face the fact that he, too, will be stuck with his inventory."

I'd like to conclude with a personal testimony.

We were on our way to Madagascar and, in order to save on airline tickets, we were booked on a charter flight leaving from Zurich. During one rather long layover at an airport, we talked to two Swiss gentlemen who looked like sportsmen. At least, they were loaded down with photographic equipment.

"You're going to take pictures of animals?"

"We're going to try to. We're in the fur business, and so we decided to see what the animals look like when they're alive."

"How's the fur business nowadays?"

"Not bad. Profits increase every year—"

"Except for one fur," the second man interrupted. "Seals. No one is buying sealskin coats any more."

"It's no wonder," the first man added. "You've no idea of the campaign that they're mounting in the newspapers and magazines against seal furs. Maybe you've seen the articles in *Paris-Match*?"

Indeed I had, since I had had a hand in them.

"It's gotten so bad that no woman would be caught dead in a sealskin coat! If you're interested, I can let you have a whole load of them at eighty percent off the retail price."

We all laughed.

The problem of protecting the spotted cats is similar to that of the seals. Hunting and poaching of these animals can be stopped only by putting a stop to consumer demand for these furs. Therefore, if the slaughter is to be stopped, it can be stopped only by informing the public.

There are furriers who protest that "There have never been as many panthers in Africa as there are now." And "If the animals are killed so brutally, it is the fault of the consumer, who insists on having beautiful furs." In the face of such protestations, conservation organizations have tried to devise a method of dealing with the problem of how to dispose of existing stockpiles of furs. For—and there are many furriers concerned about nature who will agree—some fur traders have truly enormous stocks.

This rather delicate question was put to Sir Peter Scott, Secretary General of the World Wildlife Fund. This was his reply to the fur trade: "It's simply too bad. Public opinion has turned against you. Maybe the only thing for you to do is to burn your stock, and then try to collect the insurance. However, I have a better suggestion. In order to find a use for these skins without encouraging people to buy more of them, you might consider donating a limited number of coats to museums. They could be used, for example, in exhibits of the history of fashion—as bird feathers are being used. There could even be a plaque with the donor's name on it."

The important thing now, it seems to me, is to maintain public pressure on the exploiters of nature. And that can be done only by the constant dissemination of information to the public.

The role of women

In several countries, the public has become aware of the necessity for animal conservation. Some very influential American magazines, such as *Vogue* and *Harper's Bazaar*, have explained the problem to their readers and declared that they would "no longer accept advertising for furs." Women, particularly, have been in the forefront of the battle. When such personalities as Princess Grace of Monaco, Mia Farrow, Virginia McKenna, and Elizabeth Taylor refuse to wear leopard skin coats, it is a very good sign indeed. And when one of France's most important newspapers, *Le Figaro*, tells us that 133,064 ocelot skins were imported into the United States, of which 91,226 came from Brazil and 23,823 from Colombia, we can understand the need for such stands by women in the public eye. By the same token, we can only applaud when Princess Beatrix of the Netherlands, speaking in London, gives her public support to the W.W.F. resolution asking all women, furriers, and fashion magazines to bring to a halt "all commerce in the skins of endangered species."

It is, we think, the dawn of a great movement in favor of nature.

An unhappy ending that almost was

We had been in French Guiana for a month, wandering along the wild and fascinating coast of that country. One day, we visited Saint Laurent du Maroni. As we drove slowly through an alleyway in the old port, we saw three Indians standing in a group, engaged in excited discussion.

Nadine saw it first. "Look, Christian! Look at that animal! Let's go closer."

The three Indians were, in fact, standing around a strange animal whose paws were tied to a piece of wood.

I shut off the engine and we got out.

Opposite: The sloth is one of the most beguiling creatures of the jungle. In French Guiana, these animals are called sheep sloths because of their wooly coats. This sloth lived with us for nine days. His name was Isidore.

Isidore in his usual sleeping place. We fed him branches from the canon-tree every day. In less than a week he was completely tame and understood that we were his friends.

It's just like the one that we stole from the base at Korou,"* Nadine pointed out. "Isn't it cute?"

It was an unau, or two-toed sloth—an herbivorous mammal of the jungle who is inoffensive and little known.

---

*Five days earlier, we had visited a military base at Korou. The firemen there had a sloth in the firehouse. Using the excuse that we wanted to photograph the animal in its natural habitat, we borrowed it for a while, telling ourselves that we simply wanted to take it for a walk. One of the officers caught up with us. "Look, take the animal and turn it loose somewhere. Don't bring it back to the camp. It will only die there." And that is exactly what we did.

Isidore liked to be carried. Notice his long claws. Not once did he ever scratch us, or even try to. This peaceable animal is hunted, eaten, and his skin stuffed for sale to tourists.

The situation was explained to us, through gestures, in less time than it takes to write about it. The Indians had found the sloth on the highway. It had been crossing the roadway—which is a desert, stinking of oil, passing through the dense vegetation inhabited by the animals. One man, afraid of being scratched, had picked the sloth up by its shoulders and held it at arm's length. Another had cut a small branch and tied the animal's paws to it. Fortunately, the man had not thought to cut the sloth's claws to the quick, to keep it from scratching. We had already seen that done twice in Guiana.

The sloth had been tied to the branch for three days and three nights without a drop of water, without a single leaf to eat, and without

Opposite: These Indians, when they understood that we wanted Isidore in order to set him free, thought we were crazy.

Above and below: Like the giant panda (above) and the lemur of Madagascar (below), the sloth seems to fascinate the general public. We always get a very high rating when our television broadcasts have to do with these animals.

Double page following: We are not fighting only to protect animals. We are fighting to preserve nature in all its beauty and its harmony, which is indispensable to human happiness.

being able to move its paws. The Indians announced that they intended to cook the animal for their dinner.

Nadine was horrified. The animal was looking at her wide-eyed, as though it understood what was happening and where its chance of salvation lay. I hesitated for a long time. To buy an animal is to give it a commercial value. To call the police—if they would come—would only prolong the animal's misery. And to try to persuade the Indians to turn the animal loose would only provoke a storm of laughter. The idea of throwing away good meat would have been regarded by them as proof positive that all white men are crazy. Yet, we simply could not just walk away and leave the animal with the Indians. We talked and haggled for ten minutes. Finally, we bought it, for next to nothing: the worth of an animal's life when hundreds of his species die every year over wood fires.

As quickly as we could, we took the sloth and stole away like thieves. The first night, the sloth found its favorite sleeping place in our vehicle: rolled up inside the steering wheel. The next day we christened him Isidore. We had decided that we would keep him for a week, and then turn him loose deep in the jungle, at the tree favored by sloths: the canon tree, so called by the natives because, if burned, the wood of the tree explodes.

Isidore very quickly adjusted to his new situation. The first two days, he obviously suffered from stiffness in the joints of his paws. But an abundance of leaves, water whenever he was thirsty, and the opportunity to sleep almost constantly soon restored him to good health.

We ended up keeping Isidore with us for nine days, but without pampering him or trying to accustom him to the presence of humans. Even so, not once did he show the slightest signs of fear or hostility, or try to use his claws on us.

The day that we left French Guiana, I went deep into the bush with Isidore in my arms. His head was over my shoulder, and his eyes were fixed on Nadine who was following me. Finally, I discovered a canon tree's soft, light trunk. It had the diameter of a good-sized telephone pole: the ideal size for a sloth's paws.

Isidore understood immediately. Without even looking back, he put his long paws around the tree and slowly climbed toward the top of the tree, toward the tender green leaves. Toward his natural habitat.

Millions of dollars

The problem is simple. On the one hand, there is nature in danger. On the other hand, there is the means to save nature: the World Wildlife

Fund. The results obtained by the Fund are spectacular. An enormous amount of land has been turned into parks and preserves. There have been cities, jungles, and islands saved through the determination of a few men. A great deal has already been accomplished. And the world has become aware of the existence and purpose of the W.W.F.

When we are spending billions to send expeditions to uninhabited planets, tens of billions in ruinous wars, is it too much to hope, as Prince Bernhard of the Netherlands has asked, that we will be able somewhere to find a few millions for the conservation of our own planet? "Man," the prince continued, "surely has the ability to halt the spread of deserts and to do away with piles of garbage."

There are commercial interests that spend tens of millions of dollars to destroy our environment. We can only protect and restore the planet by the same means; that is, by spending tens of millions of dollars.

Obviously, we will never succeed in preserving all the endangered species. I am nonetheless optimistic. There is a strong movement everywhere to make up for the mistakes that we have made. The race against death has begun. Let us hope that we have not started too late.

One morning in Malaysia, we had just returned, with Ken Skriven,

Happiness is living with wild animals. This is possible only in the animal's habitat, for a short period of time. And then only if care is taken not to domesticate the animal to such an extent that he becomes dependent on man.

from a night spent filming the luth turtles. We had been particularly fascinated by the painful efforts of one of these giant marine turtles to return to the sea after laying her eggs.

The sun had not yet risen. The sand was cool. And the struggling turtle was forced to stop every five or six feet to rest.

When the turtle finally reached the stretch of damp sand next to the water, I had a crazy thought. What if this ancient animal, this testimony to the beginnings of creation, that animal whose species existed before the appearance of man, was proof that the whole history of the world, from the beginning to the present day, was nothing more than an incredible error. What if the end product of evolution, the human being—the species who has now reached its point of no return—is nothing more than a cosmic prank?

Then, as I watched the turtle slowly, finally entering the water, as though to return to her own and our own origins, a bird landed on my shoulder. I could feel its tiny paws on my skin. And suddenly, I found hope again. The thought of a cosmic hoax disappeared from my mind.

I felt Ken's hand on my shoulder, shaking me. I had dozed off on the sand. I had dreamed the whole thing.

Protecting nature means protecting the beauty and surprises of life. The zebras above are standing in that unexpected position so as to be able to spot any nearby predators. The gnu in the photograph below and the elephants opposite adopt the same tactic. In each instance, the animals take up this position generally during the hottest hours of the day.

Living statues

In June 1973, we reached the Marquesas Islands. We had crossed the 1,300 miles of open sea from Tahiti without encountering the least contrary wind, the least squall. We spent most of our time lying like lizards in the sun, as though our cinnamon-colored skin had need of further tanning. Just as the freighter reached the port, a storm broke. We had just enough time to grab our equipment, get off the ship, and run to the expedition's office before it began to rain in earnest. As it was, we were soaked to the skin.

Two days later, it was still raining. Since our stay in Nuku Hiva was going to be relatively short, we decided to leave, rain or no rain, on horseback in search of the last Tiki statues.

That same evening, with the help of the inhabitants of the island, we found three statues. They were no more than six feet in height and sculpted from black lava. I took a series of photographs of the smiling, round-eyed statues, which would be used for an article. These statues are dangerous for some, beneficial for others, and mysterious for all.

Since we were already as wet as we could be, the rain no longer mattered. We sat on stools, looking at the last Tikis of the Marquesas Islands. "You see," I said to Nadine, "to me, it is as important to save the last rhinoceroses as it is to save the last Tiki statues. A masterpiece of nature is as precious as a masterpiece created by a human being. The Vanoise National Park is as important to man's happiness as the Louvre."

"Yes, but the Louvre can get money when it needs some. Not much, but some. There's no money for the rhinos."

"Ah, that's where you're wrong. There's a rhinoceros project on the board at headquarters in Switzerland. And as far as statues are concerned, I prefer the living ones. Do you remember those that we photographed in Africa? The animals arranged head-to-tail? Those were certainly statues."

"Speaking of the African sun, maybe we should get back to the village. But I like your image of animals as statues." Nadine smiled. "Didn't I hear Sir Peter Scott once say the same thing?"

The return to camp

It would be night in less than an hour, and we were still driving along Lake Manyara in Tanzania.

On the other side of the world, at that very moment, in the Corbett

Preserve, a tiger was stretching. Her forepaws were placed far in front of her body, and her hind paws seemed to drag behind her. She yawned, her pink tongue lolling in her mouth. Then, with the underside of her right paw, she began washing her long white whiskers.

In an hour, the tiger would stretch out on a rock next to a waterhole. Then, silent and stately as a queen, she would return to the bush where three cubs, like balls of golden wool, were waiting for her.

Thousands of miles from Corbett, a luth turtle was dragging its damp shell up a dune where she would dig a hole for her eggs. Some unknown force within her had enabled her to find, along the endless coast of South America, the exact spot in Guiana where, seven years earlier, she had been saved by chance from the voracious beak of a frigate bird. Deep in the jungle, in the fork of a great tree, a sloth was sleeping. In other jungles in other places, herds of elephants would also sleep. Like thousands of other animals born on a planet teeming with billions of human beings, they are, for the moment, left in peace. But for how long?

We mentioned driving alongside the lake. Mohodja lit a cigarette and handed it to Nadine, then took one for himself. The weather was cool, the sunset lovely. All three of us were silent, content. We could see blue mountains at the horizon. A flock of white pelicans, skimming the surface of the water, wheeled in perfect order toward their chosen sleeping place. The locusts were launching into their strident evening concert.

It had been a long, hot day but an exciting one. Nadine had been successful in photographing an elephant passing under an acacia tree in which a lion was sleeping. I had filmed a gray heron which, I suspected, would bring delight to millions of television viewers. To catch fish, the heron chose a shallow pool located in the sun. Then, standing in the pool, he spread his wings, creating a cool shadow with which to tempt the small fish in the pool. He had only to pick up the fishes in his beak. The shadow also allowed him to more easily distinguish his prey.

In less than ten days, we would return to Paris. We would have to pack our equipment carefully, spreading it among our suitcases and boxes so as to avoid any charges for excess weight. We would try to sleep on the plane. Then we would be there. The hassle with customs officials. The smiles of our friends. And the taste of real French bread.

I slowed down, almost stopping, to detour around a large fallen branch across the road. It had not been there in the morning. Our friends, the elephants, had no doubt used the same trail.

Double page following: An extraordinary spectacle: the horns of the fourth buffalo from the left are almost as wide as the hood of our Landrover.

Two miles further, the trail curved away from the shore to avoid a marsh. Like ebony statues on pedestals of gold, five motionless water buffalo stood facing us fifty yards away. I cut the engine and the sudden silence was deafening, as though the noise of the engine had been a barrier between us and the animals. We grabbed our cameras and began shooting. I watched Mohodja out of the corner of my eye. He smiled, and took his time telling me that one of the buffalo was the largest specimen on the preserve. He had known the buffalo for seven years. Its preferred territory was the tall grass, and, for that reason, the animal was rarely seen. It was a stroke of good luck for us to encounter the buffalo—and to see the beauty, the splendor, the visual perfection that surrounded us at that moment.

Keeping my eyes on the buffalo, I turned the ignition key and pressed gently on the accelerator. We moved forward. The soft breeze caressed our sunburned cheeks. At the end of the trail there would be fresh water to drink, a shower, and a bed.

For us, the voyage was over. But the adventure goes on.

Appendices
and glossary

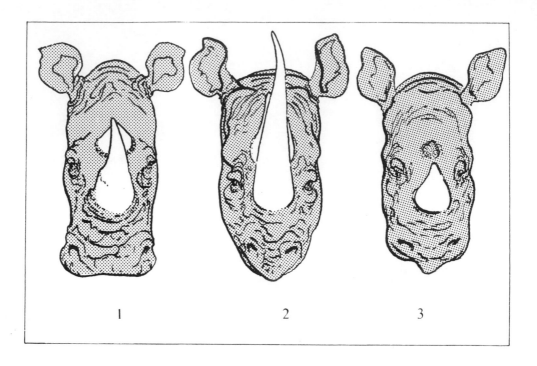

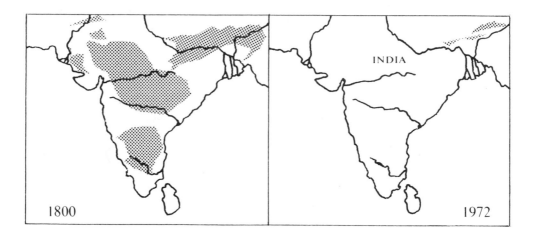

We have filmed only three of the five species of rhinoceros: the two African species, one with a wide, square snout and the other with a pointed snout. The former is popularly, and incorrectly, called the white rhino rather than the wide rhino. The third species, the Indian rhinoceros, is smaller than his African cousins.

These maps show the extent of Indian rhino territory in 1800 and in 1972. This species is now regarded as saved from extinction, but it will never regain its former numbers.

appendix I

LEGENDS THAT KILL

Tigers: "Tigers are man-eaters." Some lions, in exceptional cases, have developed a taste for human flesh; and that taste is diminished neither by age nor by infirmity. Man-eating tigers, however, are extremely rare.

Rhinoceroses: "The horn of the rhinoceros is a powerful aphrodisiac." False. This legend is not based on the phallic shape of the horn (which is composed of hair), but on the fact that the mating act of the rhinoceros may last for as long as an hour. On three occasions, I have eaten powdered rhinoceros horns without feeling the least effect. This naive belief is responsible for the almost total disappearance of the five species of rhinoceros.

Owls: "Owls are unlucky." In the Seychelles and on other islands, people bury screech owls and hoot owls alive in the sand. In some parts of Europe, peasants burn them or nail them to the doors of barns. All predatory owls are useful to man. The large-scale destruction of these birds on the highways, in traps, and with pesticides, explains their general rarity in developed countries.

Lions: "Lions hunt at night." There are two errors here. It is female lions who do the hunting. And more than seventy-five percent of the animals killed by lions are killed during the day. In Africa, and above all in India, lions who do not live on preserves are growing fewer in number every year. They are being killed by hunters. On the other hand, lions in zoos multiply rapidly. There is hardly a zoo in the world that is not trying to sell lions. It does no good to try to release these excess animals into the wild, for animals born in captivity very rarely can survive in nature.

Bats: "Bats get tangled up in human hair." False. Bats, in fact, have excellent sonar systems that allow them to avoid hitting objects in flight. If, as happens occasionally, a bat should brush against someone holding a flashlight, it is because he is trying to catch the insects attracted by the light.

Frogs: "Frogs' legs grow back when they are cut off." False. The thousands of frogs' legs that are sold every year are cut from frogs that are then released. All these animals die terrible deaths. No vertebrate has ever grown a new paw to replace one that was amputated.

Snakes: "If a snake bites you, you must suck out the venom." A completely ineffective method of treatment. The poison, if there is any, penetrates into the muscles almost instantly. Also, trying to suck out the venom is dangerous: the well-intentioned person doing the sucking may be infected by the venom if he has a sore or scratch in his mouth. In case of snakebite, lie down and send immediately for a physician. Try to determine what kind of snake was involved, so that the proper antidote may be used.

Manta rays: "Manta rays turn over fishermen's boats and eat the fishermen." False. Like many animals, manta rays have parasites. When the parasites are attached to the ray's stomach, he rids himself of them by rubbing against rocks. If they are on his back, he rubs against anything floating on the surface. Sometimes it is a tree trunk. Sometimes it is a piece of driftwood. And, by way of exception, it is sometimes a fishing boat. The boat may capsize and the fishermen fall into the water. But sharks may have been attracted by the disturbance, and these, of course, may well attack the men in the water. No manta ray has ever eaten a human being. Rays, like whales, live on plankton.

Hedgehogs and porcupines: "Hedgehogs can carry apples stuck on their quills." False—for the simple reason that a hedgehog's quills stick up only when the animal is rolled up in a ball. Photographs showing anything else are hoaxes.

"Porcupines are able to shoot their quills." False. The porcupine has no muscle capable of shooting quills. Nonetheless, this legend persists. Even the Arab word for this animal, *dropan*, testifies to the durability of this belief. *Drop* means "to shoot." The legend may originate in the fact that the porcupine sheds his quills, just as other mammals regularly shed their fur.

Hyenas: "Hyenas are hermaphroditic." False. The family groups of this animal are dominated by the female. This holds true in Africa as well as in Asia. This female is the first to rush to the defense of the family. In combat, the fur on her back rises and an organ, in the shape of a penis, sometimes appears between her hind legs. This pecularity is no doubt the basis of the legend.

Birds' eggs: "If you take away a bird's eggs, she will lay more eggs." This is occasionally true for wild birds, and never true for domesticated birds. As a general rule, a bird's nest should never be disturbed in any way, even if it is on the ground. Collecting birds' eggs, on the pretext of their educational or scientific values, should always be avoided. Even taking photographs of birds should be done only in moderation, so as to disturb the birds as little as possible.

Birds and crocodiles: "Plovers clean the teeth of crocodiles." This may be true. But, so far, no one has produced a photograph or film of this widely reported phenomenon. Nor has there been any indisputable testimony to confirm these reports.

Because furriers insist on furs in excellent condition, poachers kill leopards in a particularly horrifying way. The animal is trapped and then tied, spread-eagle, in its cage. A bar of iron is then inserted into the leopard's anus and pushed forward until it reaches its lungs. Sometimes the bar is heated until it is red-hot. Sometimes these cats are hanged. Only the removal of all spotted furs from the market can put a stop to this slaughter.

appendix II

LETTER FROM A MAN-EATER

In April, 1973, *Le Figaro* published a news item about a man-eating tiger in India who, it was reported, had attacked a bee keeper. The tiger's answer was published in the same newspaper on May 3, 1973:

I am taking the liberty of writing to you in order to respond to an article recently published in your newspaper on the subject of man-eaters.

Allow me to introduce myself. I am a very old tiger. I live alone, deep in the jungle on Corbett Preserve, not far from New Delhi. I have no near neighbors. In my grandfather's time, there were some 40,000 of us throughout India. Today, there are only about 1,800 of us still alive.

Ordinarily, I eat antelope; but it happens occasionally that I must be content with a hare, or a tough old monkey, or even a frog. I usually sleep during the day and hunt at night. I say "usually" because I am often disturbed by tourists, riding on elephants, who want to take pictures of me.

I have no natural enemies in the jungle. I am not afraid even of the elephants. I fear only one thing—the same thing that all the other animals fear: human beings. You may then imagine my astonishment and indignation when such a respected newspaper as yours reports that tigers are eating bee keepers.

Perhaps you will allow me to explain in some detail. In Sundarbans, in the east of India, hunters have exterminated the antelope which, in happier days, were our source of food. For that reason, a few humans in that area were eaten by elderly tigers who were unable to find any other game. I can assure you, however, that as a general rule, felines are frightened by odors, noises, traps, poisons, and highly developed weapons; and that tigers, the last tigers, are much less dangerous than certain human beings.

I am aware that certain preserves are going to be set aside for our exclusive use. Madam Indira Gandhi is encouraging and participating in

Our headlights are on a female tiger with her paw in a trap. I got out of the Landrover to take photographs, but I was careful to stay out of the light and not to enter the tiger's security zone.

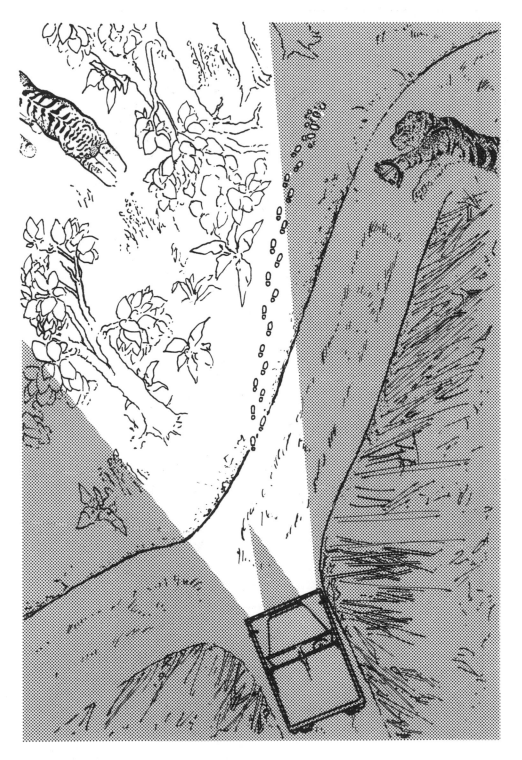

As we backed away from the tiger, our headlights shone on the male tiger only a few yards away. He had certainly seen my silhouette while I was taking pictures but, for some reason, he did not attack.

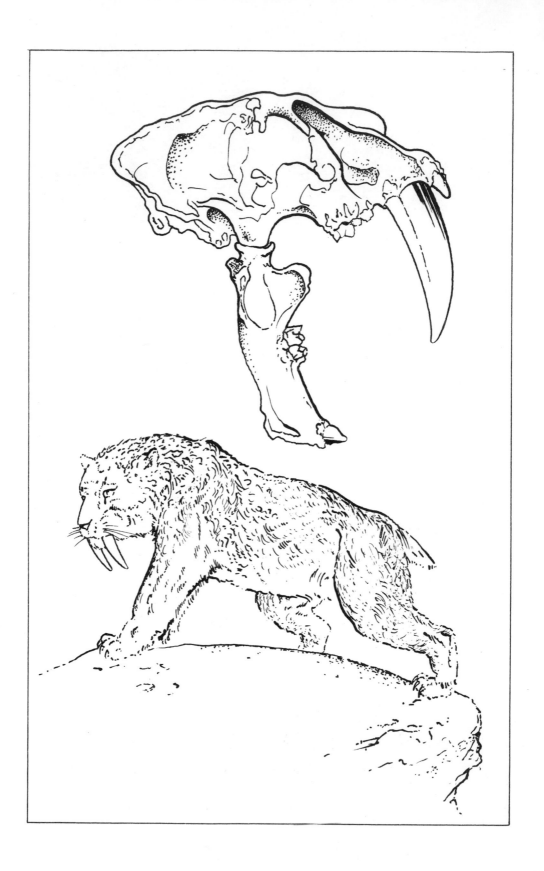

Above: As can be seen from above, every tiger has individual markings on its face, and no two adult tigers are identical. This characteristic makes it possible for researches to identify individual tigers without marking them artificially.

Opposite: The present-day tiger is descended from a feline with enormous upper canines known as the sabre-toothed tiger. This animal, also called Machairodus, lived at the end of the Tertiary period.

this conservation program, which will result perhaps in the reestablishment of the necessary equilibrium in nature.* You may rest assured,

---

*The international campaign for the protection of the last tigers, organized by the World Wildlife Fund. All requests for information should be addressed to this newspaper.

however, that as long as the so-called civilized countries, such as France, allow the sale of feline skins, nothing will be able to put a halt to the poaching, sale, and slaughter of tigers and other fur-bearing animals.

I know whereof I speak. My grandfather, my own parents, my two uncles, all of my neighbors, and my mother-in-law all were killed for the sake of their skins. I will not even mention the death, at a poisoned water hole, of my last wife, and the subsequent death, of thirst, of her three cubs in the underbrush.

At that rate, it seems likely that none of us will survive.

Last year, a cinematographer and his wife came here in order to make films and take photographs of me. I was somewhat frightened because they used a telescopic lens, which resembled the barrel of a large gun. After two weeks, when I was convinced that they had no weapons and that they kept their distance, I pretended to ignore them. They shot me from every possible angle, as though I were a movie star. Then, one night, they left, taking with them their fire, their smell of gasoline, and their films.

I hope one day to see these films on television. You will then realize that the abominable "man-eating tigers" of your article are only the exceptions to the rule. Perhaps you will realize that we, too, have a right to life; that the sale of our skins is an atrocity; and that, finally, if we should disappear altogether in the forseeable future, no one will ever be able to hear us roar, or see us, or even film us in our jungle—which, I should point out, is also your jungle.

In closing, I can only add that I have observed the ability of your species in ruling the earth, in building new and larger automobiles, in inventing new weapons, and even in sending new satellites into orbit. But I have never heard it said that you are capable of creating anything—not even a flower, a bird, or a tiger.

Letter delivered from India by Christian Zuber

appendix III

In the line of equipment, we try to chose things that are sturdy, light, and of high quality. If, for reasons that are not our responsibility, this equipment disappoints us, we say so. By the same token, if it satisfies us, we say that also. When we mention brand names, it is our way of thanking the manufacturers for having provided us with first-quality equipment.

Our cinematographic equipment is all checked before and after each expedition, as is our photographic equipment. Our underwater cameras are tested in swimming pools. Our lights are tested in the Bois de Boulogne in Paris—to the astonishment of the police. And, since some of our lens are specially made (400 to 600 mm), we do a thorough check of every technical detail.

Our equipment is spread out among a number of small aluminum suitcases. For a typical voyage, we carry nine of these suitcases. For a very important expedition, we carry fourteen. Then, of course, there are our personal effects.

For customs officials, we provide dozens of lists typed on letter-head stationery and fortified with various stamps and seals. Nothing seems to impress the official mind more than a piece of paper that has been stamped. Press cards, on the other hand, can be two-edged swords. Sometimes, we hide ours in our diving equipment.

We never carry weapons. A pen-style rocket gun (for colors, smoke-screens, explosions) gives us a feeling of security in the jungle because it sometimes happens that an animal that has been disturbed or unintentionally provoked will attack. (It is worth repeating once more that, in general, all wild animals will run away from human beings.) It is also worth remembering that, in certain parts of the world, there are people who will kill you in order to get your gun. This used to happen rarely, but nowadays it seems to be on the increase. In brief, our weapons are our cameras.

Cameras:

>Arriflex 16 mm electric. Battery belt.
>Lens: 10, 25, 50, 100, 300, and 600 mm.
>Zoom: 12, 120 Angenieux.
>Macro Kilar: Kinoptic.
>Paillard Bolex 16 mm with zoom.
>Underwater camera: Paillard in a Boisnard-Guiter case.

Photographic equipment:

>Nikon. F.II with fast viewfinder.
>Lens: 28, 35, 85, 200, 400, 600 mm.
>Macro Nikor. 55 mm.
>Novoflex 400 mm with Leitz lens.
>Videlux (wide-angle width on two transparencies).
>Nikonos. Underwater cameras.
>Rolleimarin. Two flashlights.

Sound equipment:

>Nagra tape recorder.
>Tapes, speed 19.
>Ultra-directional microphones.

Accessories:

>Two Japanese walkie-talkies.
>Tripods. Three different makes.
>Power cells: Weston Master and Lunasix.

Miscellaneous:

>Complete repair kit.
>Fishing equipment. Mirrors.
>Flares.
>Notebooks.
>Photographs of earlier expeditions.
>Photographs of exotic animals.
>Two film-conferences in color.

Film:

>Ektachrome 7255.
>By way of exception, Kodachrome II (underwater).
>Same film for photography, especially Kodachrome II.

The golden rule of journalism: Always press the button when something is happening—even if the conditions are bad, the camera is not properly adjusted, or there is danger. The important thing is to bring back film no matter what happens. Never "set up" a film or a photograph. And always respect your subject, whether it is a man or an animal.

A final detail: unlike many other reporters, we do not use the shotgun technique in shooting film or in taking photographs. We do not shoot miles of film and thousands of photos and then pick the few good ones. We learned in Morocco to economize on film.

Our dream: thanks to the satellites in orbit and to the equipment that will certainly appear in the foreseeable future, we hope to be able (our finances permitting) to do what the astronauts do: to explore and report *live* to the television audience on what is happening to us. When that day comes, if it is not already too late, television will indeed be in a position to save nature.

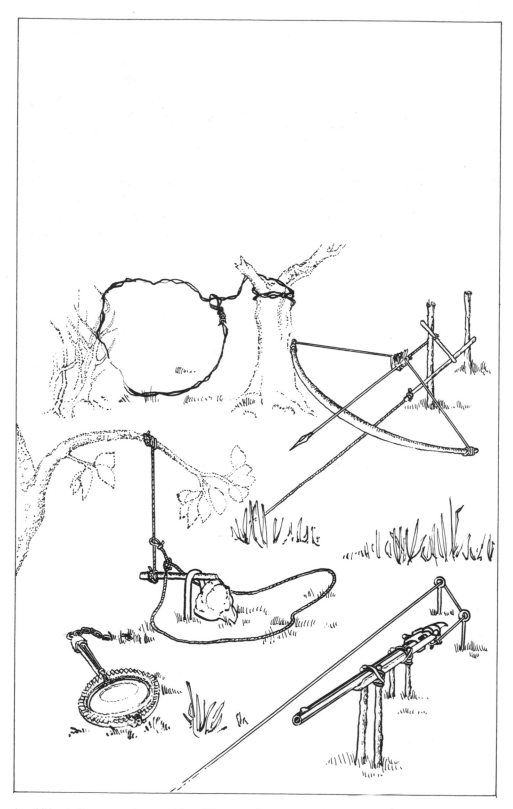

In addition to firearms, poison, and forest fires, poachers use a variety of traps. Even in the most remote areas, one finds at least one evidence of civilization: metal traps for capturing animals.

appendix IV

Below is a very incomplete list of the mammals, birds, and reptiles that are either extinct or in danger of becoming extinct. These are not animals that are disappearing because of natural causes. They are all animals exterminated by man.

A complete list would run to almost 900 species. We have intentionally cut down the list to make it more manageable.

The information in the list is taken from the *Red Data Book*, published by the I.U.C.N. The reader will get some idea of the work done by the three major international organizations—all nongovernmental and therefore apolitical—that have been working to protect nature for many years: I.C.P.B. (International Council for the Protection of Birds, founded in 1922); I.U.C.N. (International Union for Conservation of Nature, founded in 1948); and W.W.F. (World Wildlife Fund). The mission of the latter is to collect the funds necessary for the operation of other organizations and to the realization of over 1,600 projects for saveguarding nature throughout the world.

This work, ideally, should be undertaken in close collaboration with the general public. But, as Paul Geroudet has remarked, "Most of our contemporaries could not care less that whales, lemurs, and leopards are disappearing. Some people think that economic development is more important than the survival of this or that species. This kind of short-sighted egoism will lead to destruction of another kind that we cannot even imagine." The conservation of endangered animal species is therefore an absolute necessity for the future of life on earth.

It is our hope that the following list will not grow in years to come. We may even hope that it will grow shorter rather than longer, thanks to the activities of the international conservation organizations and, finally, thanks to you, the readers of this book.

NORTH AMERICA

BLACK-FOOTED FERRET *(Mustela nigripes).* The rarest of the North American mammals.

SOUTHERN SEA OTTER *(Enhydra lutris nereis).* There are only 850 to 900 specimens left along the coast. There is little chance of saving this species.

EASTERN COUGAR *(Felis concolor cougar).* Now extinct in most of its habitat.

ATLANTIC WALRUS *(Odobenus rosmarus).* Some herds are near extinction. The species can no longer tolerate commercial exploitation.

CARIBBEAN MONK SEAL *(Monachus tropicalis).* Now extremely rare.

BARREN GROUND GRIZZLY BEAR *(Ursus arctos).* Has disappeared from most of the continent. It must be saved quickly if it is to survive at all.

POLAR BEAR *(Thalarctos (Ursus) maritimus).* An international plan is intended to save this species, which is threatened with imminent extinction.

UTAH PRAIRIE DOG *(Cynomys parvidens).* Once very large, the prairie-dog population is diminishing alarmingly.

CURIERS' HUTIA AND DOMINICAN HUTIA *(Plagiodontia aedium et P. hylaeum)* Native to the Dominican Republic and Haiti, this animal has become very rare.

KEY DEER *(Odocoileus virginianus clarium).* Has practically disappeared from the area that it once inhabited. There are about 300 specimens in the Florida Keys.

WOOD BISON *(Bison bison athabascae).* Has narrowly escaped extinction.

EURASIA

MEDITERRANEAN MONK SEAL *(Monachus monachus).* Extinct.

SPANISH LYNX *(Felis lynx pardina).* Its disappearance is linked to the destruction of its habitat.

PRZEWALSKI'S HORSE *(Equus przewalskii).* At present, the only wild horse in the world. It has become very rare and is strictly protected.

ASIATIC WILD ASS *(Equus hemionus).* Less than 1,000 specimens.

MONGOLIAN WILD ASS *(Equus hemionus hemionus).* Very much in danger, but strictly protected.

WILD BACTRIAN CAMEL *(Camelus bactrianus).* On the way to extinction.

EUROPEAN BISON *(Bison bonasus)*. Almost extinct, it was saved after World War II.

ARABIAN ORYX *(Oryx leucoryx)*. Very rare and difficult to protect.

AFRICA

CHIMPANZEE *(Pan troglodytes)*. The pygmy subspecies *(pan troglodytes paniscus)* is little known and very rare. The species itself is diminishing in numbers.

GORILLA *(Gorilla gorilla)*. The victim of excessive hunting. The subspecies, known as the mountain gorilla *(Gorilla gorilla beringei)*, is particularly endangered.

LEOPARD *(Panthera pardus)*. Has practically disappeared in North Africa. The leopard has been victimized by excessive hunting everywhere.

MOUNTAIN ZEBRA *(Equus zebra)*. Two subspecies, the mountain zebra *(Equus zebra zebra)* and the Hartman zebra *(Equus zebra hartmannae)*, are threatened with extinction.

BLACK RHINOCEROS *(Diceros bicornis)*. Although protected on most of its territory, the black rhinoceros is in imminent danger of extinction.

NORTHERN SQUARE-LIPPED RHINOCEROS *(Ceratotherium simum cottoni)*. Almost extinct. Attempts are being made to save it in several national preserves.

GIANT SABLE ANTELOPE *(Hippotragus niger variani)*. Found only in southern Angola. Only 500 to 700 specimens remain.

SCIMITAR-HORNED ORYX *(Oryx dammah)*. An emergency situation. Reasonably abundant only in Chad.

ADDAX *(Addax nasomaculatus)*. Like the above oryx, the addax must be saved at once if it is to be saved at all.

BLACK WILDE BEEST *(Connochaetes gnou)*. Once on the verge of extinction, the black wilde beest now seems assured of survival.

SLENDER-HORNED GAZELLE *(Gazella leptoceros)*. This gazelle is protected nowhere and is extremely vulnerable.

DUGONG *(Dugong dugon)*. Also found along the coasts of southern Asia. The number of dugongs is diminishing everywhere.

MADAGASCAR

All the lemurs of Madagascar are considerably fewer than they once were. Their survival is linked to the preservation of their natural habitat. Among the most spectacular lemurs are:

INDRI *(Indri indri)*. Very vulnerable because its territory is limited.

AYE-AYE *(Daubentonia madagascariensis)*. Perhaps the rarest and most remarkable of the mammals.

SOUTH AMERICA

GIANT OTTER *(Pteronura brasiliensis)*. Declining because of its exceptionally beautiful fur.

VICUNA *(Vicugna vicugna)*. Fewer than 1,000 specimens.

GIANT ANTEATER *(Myrmecophaga tridactyla)*. Becomes fewer in number wherever humans move in.

MOUNTAIN TAPIR *(Tapirus pinchaque)*. The number of these animals is declining rapidly. In urgent need of being saved.

CHILEAN PUDU *(Pudu pudu)*. Very rare. Protected.

SOUTHERN ASIA

ORANGUTAN *(Pongo pygmaeus)*. On the verge of extinction. No specimens may be captured.

GIANT PANDA *(Ailuropoda melanoleuca)* Very rare, and strictly protected.

ASIATIC LION *(Panthera leo persica)*. Found only in the Gir jungle, which is strictly protected.

TIGER *(Panthera tigris)*. Certain geographical races of tiger have become extremely rare. Very much an endangered species.

BROW-ANTLERED DEER *(Cervus eldi)*. In danger of extinction over most of its territory.

RYUKYU SIKA *(Cervus nippon keramae)*. Endangered in its country of origin.

PÈRE DAVID'S DEER *(Elaphurus davidianus)*. Extinct except for specimens in captivity.

ASIATIC BUFFALO *(Bubalus bubalis)*. Diminishing everywhere.

ANOA *(Anoa depressicornis)*. A native of Celebes, the anoa's future is very much in doubt.

KOUPREY *(Bos sauveli)*. Probably extinct at the present time.

GAUR *(Bos gaurus)*. Rare; to be saved in the preserves.

SUMATRAN SEROW *(Capricornis sumatraensis)*. Becoming extinct.

JAPANESE SEROW *(Capricornis crispus)*. Survives in the preserves, where there are about 1,500 specimens.

THE PACIFIC ISLANDS

HAWAIIAN MONK SEAL *(Monachus schauinslandi)*. Protected, but there are no more than 1,500 specimens.

AUSTRALIA and TASMANIA

THYLACINE *(Thylacinus cynocephalus)*. This animal no longer exists on the Australian continent, but survives in a preserve in Tasmania where it is strictly protected.

LEADBEATER'S POSSUM *(Gymnobelideus leadbeateri)*. Once thought to be extinct. There are specimens in the state of Victoria, where they are protected.

CRESCENT NAIL-TAILED WALLABY *(Onychogalea lunata)*. The rarest of the kangaroos. Not protected.

ANTARCTICA

ROSS SEAL *(Ommatophoca rossi)*. One of the very rare seals. Strictly protected.

The cetaceans—whales, porpoises, and even the dolphins—have practically disappeared from the Northern Hemisphere. Now they are being hunted mercilessly in Antarctica. In 1972, almost 8,200 dolphins were killed, primarily by Russian and Japanese fishermen. The slaughter continues today.

A FEW EXAMPLES OF ENDANGERED SPECIES OF BIRDS

SHORT-TAILED ALBATROSS *(Diomedea albatrus)*. One of the rarest birds in the world.

DIABLOTIN *(Pterodroma hasitata)*. The only remaining colony is in Haiti.

CAHOW *(Pterodroma cahow)*. Extremely endangered.

ABBOT'S BOOBY *(Sula abbotti)*. There are 2,000 surviving couples on Christmas Island.

KING SHAG *(Phalacrocorax c. carunculatus)*. Saved at the very last minute.

LITTLE BITTERN *(Ixobrychus minutus novaeze landiae)*. Probably extinct.

CHINESE EGRET *(Egretta eulophotes)*. Still a victim of the accessories industry, the egret has become extremely rare.

JAPANESE WHITE STORK *(Ciconia c. boyciana)*. On the verge of extinction and in urgent need of being saved.

JAPANESE CRESTED IBIS *(Nipponia nippon)*. Almost extinct. There are only nine surviving specimens.

HAWAIIAN OR NENE GOOSE *(Branta sandvicensis)*. An example of a species preserved through the efforts of the International Union for Conservation of Nature.

LAYSAN DUCK *(Anas laysanensis).* A very endangered species, preserved in captivity.

CALIFORNIA CONDOR *(Gymnogyps californianus).* Apparently doomed to extinction.

AFRICAN LAMMERGEYER *(Gypaëtus barbatus meridionalis).* A beautiful bird in need of protection. There are survivors in Corsica and in the Pyrenees.

MONKEY-EATING EAGLE *(Pithecophaga jefferyi).* Disappearing because so many have been captured for zoos. It should be forbidden by law to keep eagles in captivity.

SPANISH IMPERIAL EAGLE *(Aquila heliaca aldaberti).* Has disappeared from most of its former territory.

MAURITIUS KESTREL *(Falco punctatus).* Once very common, this bird has practically disappeared. It may be the rarest bird in the world.

MARIANAS MEGAPODE AND PALAU MEGAPODE *(Megapodius laperouse).* Requires strict protection.

ATTWATERS' PRAIRIE CHICKEN AND GREATER PRAIRIE CHICKEN *(Tympanuchus cupido).* Diminishing because of the destruction of its habitat.

PHEASANTS. Almost all species are threatened in the wild. They reproduce in captivity.

WHOOPING CRANE *(Grus americana).* Among the rarest birds in the world. A preservation program is under way.

TAKAHE *(Notornis mantelli).* A very interesting bird that every effort is being made to save.

KAGU *(Rhynochetos jubatus).* A preservation program is under way.

ESKIMO CURLEW *(Numenius borealis).* A difficult species to save.

KAKAPO OWL PARROT *(Strigops hobrophilus).* On the brink of extinction.

GROUND PARROT *(Pezoporus wallicus).* Very much in danger.

SOUTH PACIFIC PARAKEET *(Cyanoramphus).* Several species are already extinct.

PRINCE RUSPOLI'S TURACO *(Touraco ruspolii).* On the verge of disappearing.

SEYCHELLES OWL *(Otus insularis).* On the verge of disappearing.

IVORY-BILLED WOODPECKER *(Campephilus principalis).* Very uncertain future. There are perhaps five survivors.

IMPERIAL WOODPECKER *(Campephilus imperialis).* Desperate situation.

Many species and subspecies of sparrow are also in danger of disappearing—especially in the southwest of France, where hunting has been done commercially.

REPTILES

TUATARA *(Sphenodon punctatus)*. A very old reptile. Strictly protected.

GIANT GALAPAGOS TURTLE *(Testudo elephantopus)*. Survivors are protected by law, as they are in the Seychelles.

GREEN TURTLE *(Chelonia mydas)*. Soon there will not be enough of these turtles to satisfy commercial requirements.

HAWKSBILL TURTLE *(Eretmochelys imbricata)*. Very discouraging outlook.

LUTH TURTLE *(Dermochelys coriacea)*. Distributed unevenly over its former territory. It is a threatened species, surviving in Malaysia.

CUBAN CROCODILE *(Crocodylus rhombifer)*. Protected on preserves.

GALAPAGOS LAND IGUANAS *(Conolophus subcristatus* and *pollidus)*. The survival of the iguana is linked to the availability of its food: vegetation, which must be protected.

KOMODO DRAGON OR KOMODO ISLAND MONITOR *(Varanus komodoensis)*. Protected in a very large preserve. Cannot be exported.

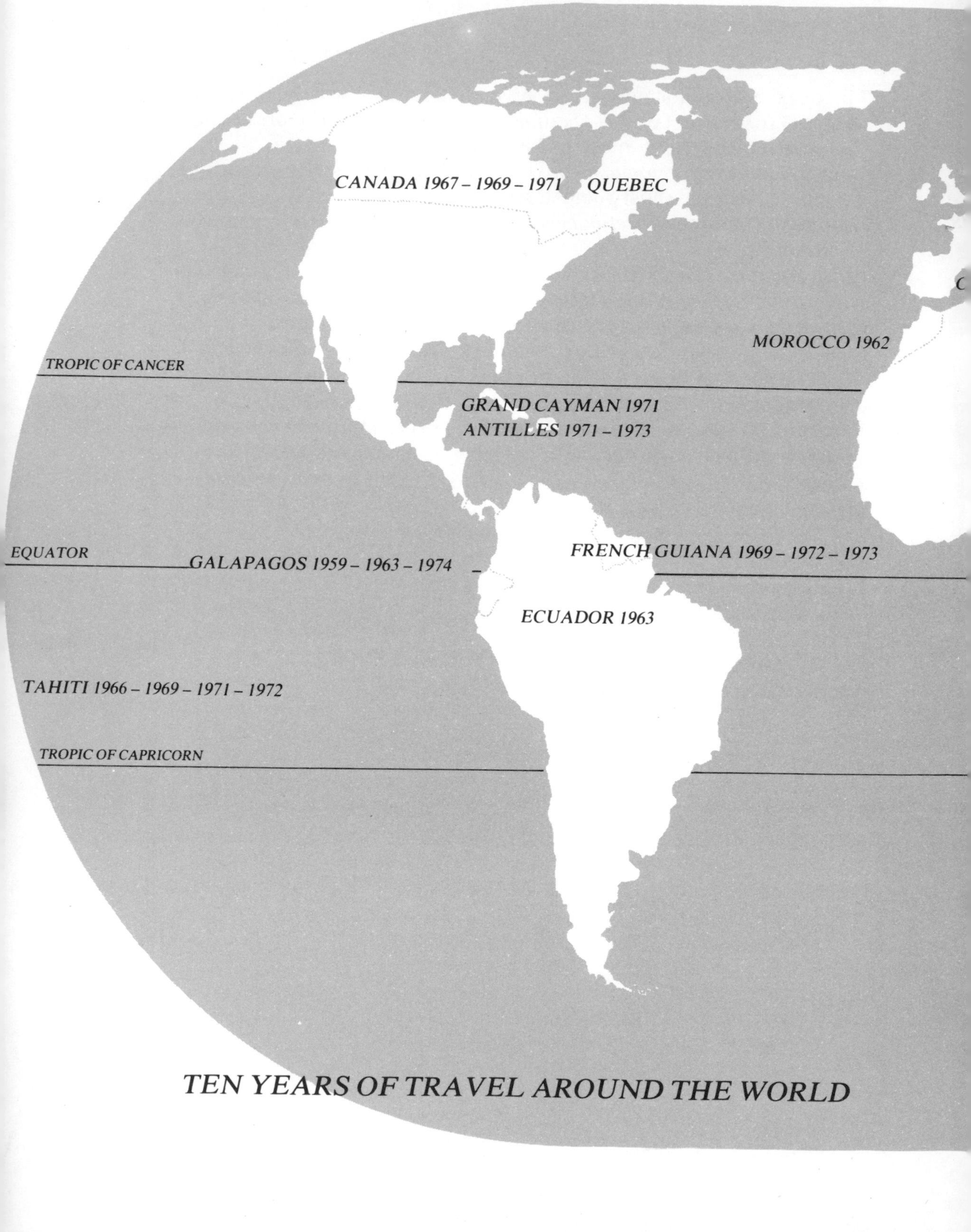

CANADA 1967 – 1969 – 1971   QUEBEC

MOROCCO 1962

TROPIC OF CANCER

GRAND CAYMAN 1971
ANTILLES 1971 – 1973

EQUATOR   GALAPAGOS 1959 – 1963 – 1974   FRENCH GUIANA 1969 – 1972 – 1973

ECUADOR 1963

TAHITI 1966 – 1969 – 1971 – 1972

TROPIC OF CAPRICORN

TEN YEARS OF TRAVEL AROUND THE WORLD

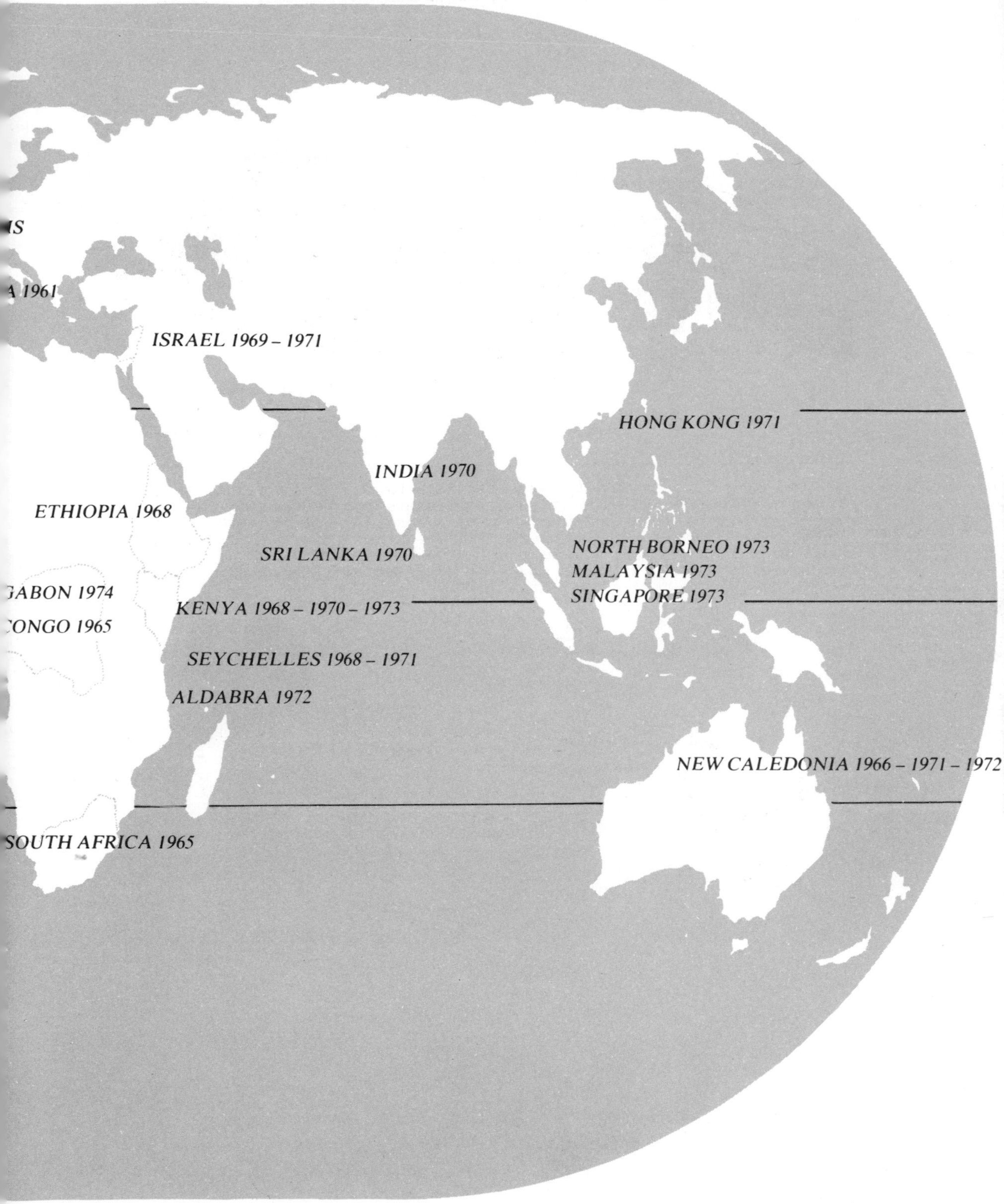

IS

A 1961

ISRAEL 1969 – 1971

HONG KONG 1971

INDIA 1970

ETHIOPIA 1968

NORTH BORNEO 1973
MALAYSIA 1973
SINGAPORE 1973

SRI LANKA 1970

GABON 1974

KENYA 1968 – 1970 – 1973

CONGO 1965

SEYCHELLES 1968 – 1971

ALDABRA 1972

NEW CALEDONIA 1966 – 1971 – 1972

SOUTH AFRICA 1965

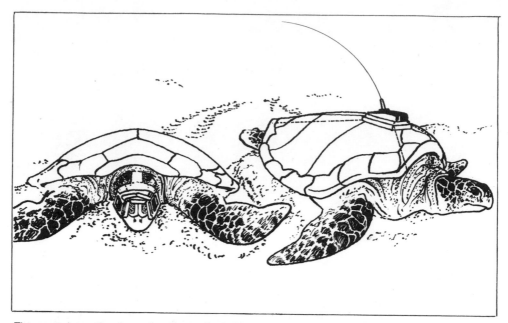

The mysterious migrations of marine turtles have been studied by Dr. D. Ehrenfeld and Dr. A. Carr. The use of a radio transmitter—as was used in studying elephants, lions, reindeer, and other large animals—allowed them to follow the movements of turtles, although the signals from the transmitter were received only when the turtle surfaced in order to breathe. Experiments with eyeglasses and interchangeable lens that were lighter or darker in hue, revealed that these marine animals, like migratory birds, steered themselves by the stars at night. When the sky was cloudy, they traveled at a considerably slower pace.

The disappearance of the dodo is due at least indirectly to the human presence. The importation of rhesus monkeys from India brought about, in just a few years' time, the destruction, if not of the birds themselves, at least of their eggs. The frequency with which the dodo appears in paintings would seem to indicate that a few of these birds may have been brought back to Holland, alive, by seamen.

Glossary of terms

ALBINO

Albinism (from the Latin *albus*, white) is a congenital anomaly that involves a diminution or absence of coloring agent in the skin, hair, scales, and even the eyes. There are albinos among almost all species of animals. *Melanism*, which is the opposite of *albinism*, involves an accumulation of dark coloring agents. Thus, in the same litter of leopards, some of the cubs may be spotted and others entirely black.

AMBLE

A four-legged animal's method of moving so that the legs on either side are lifted together. The elephant, giraffe, and camel all amble. Some horses, after much training, are able to amble. This is uncomfortable for a rider, since the latter's body shifts from side to side with each step.

BIOTOPE

From the Greek *bios*, life, and *topos*, place. The area or place in which a species lives. The destruction of the biotope (forest, jungle, ocean bottom, marsh, etc.) is one of the chief reasons for the disappearance of many species of animals. The purchase or financing, by the W.W.F., of parks and preserves is a primary solution to the problem of preserving animal life.

BOMA

The center of a Masai village, usually surrounded by a fence, intended as a corral for young animals to protect them from attack by wild animals. The village itself is a *manyatta*.

DASSANECH

A primitive tribe of southern Ethiopia. The Dassanechs have no watches, but are aware of the planets in orbit. They live from their herds, from fishing, and from hunting. There is only one European who speaks their language.

DEINOTHERIUM

The deinotherium was not precisely an ancestor of the elephant, but rather a form of life belonging to the same ancestral tree. They were herbivores. Their tusks were small and slanted downward. Skulls and fossilized skeletons have been found at Omo, in southern Ethopia, by Dr. Yves Coppens.

DUGONG (SEA COW)

A large marine mammal of the order Sirenian which feeds on algae and underwater vegetation. It is a completely inoffensive creature. These animals utter cries that resemble human moaning. The teats are located at the level of the pectoral flippers; that is, rather far forward on the animal's body. The dugong may well be at the root of the legend of the Sirens which figure in the story of Ulysses' voyages. The order Sirenian appeared on earth in the middle of the Eocene epoch (about fifty million years ago) in Africa (Egypt) and North America.

FILAO

A tree with very light branches. It grows in sand dunes and dry areas. Its wood is used for fire and, in Polynesia, for certain kinds of sculpture.

GAVIAL

The gavial is a long-snouted crocodile found in India, along the Ganges. Fossils have been found in Africa. The gavial reaches a length of fifteen feet and feeds on fish. (*Gharial*, in Hindu, means "fish-eater.") The gavial lays its eggs on the shore, and covers each layer of eggs with a layer of sand. Gavials rarely attack human beings. Most such reports are the result of confusion between the gavial and one of its cousins, a thirty-five foot monster that lives in the sea and is quite rare.

BEE-EATER

A bird about the size of a starling, having a long beak and a long tail. It is a bright-colored bird, sometimes bright scarlet. The bee-eater feeds on insects which it captures in mid-air. It is often seem around brushfires, waiting for the insects to be driven out by the heat.

GENE

A particle of matter bearing a chromosome and determining one or more hereditary characteristics. Thus, a gene may be responsible for the color of one's hair, eyes, or skin.

GUIDE

The title of "guide" depends on the area. In Africa, a "guide" is a man who walks at the head of the line. In some places, the guide is also called a *pisteur* or a chief porter. We did not put much store in these titles during our expeditions. We were a team; and that is one of the things we enjoy most about our work.

LAMMERGEYER

The lammergeyer, like all of Europe's large vultures, has become very rare because so many of them have been killed by hunters. The lammergeyer attains a length of about forty inches and a wingspan of almost ten feet. It is a harmless bird, feeding on carrion. It breaks the bones of a dead animal by dropping them down on rocks. There are three couples still alive in the French Pyrenees, and perhaps two couples on Corsica. It is the only one of the large vultures whose tail is pointed.

LEMUR

A group of mammals, family Lemuridae, related in the distant past to the ancestors of man and the superior primates (gorillas, chimpanzees, orangutans). Lemurs are found particularly on Madagascar. The strangest lemur is the aye-aye. The largest is the indri. The lemurs all eat fruits and live in trees. They are harmless. The various species are endangered because of the threatened destruction of their biotope.

LODGE

A lodge is a guest house in the country. In the south and east of Africa, there are sumptuous lodges for the accommodation of tourists. Generally, they consist of a main building, where meals are served and entertainment provided, surrounded by bungalows for occupancy by guests. Every lodge has its half-tamed animals who confidently exhibit themselves to be photographed by the tourists.

MAHOUT

A *mahout* is the friend, pilot, and guardian of the Indian elephant. He climbs up onto the elephant by standing on the animal's right forepaw and pulling himself up to the neck, where he sits. He holds onto the elephant's right ear (almost all elephants are right-handed). The *mahout* is the elephant's pilot, but not its trainer. After an elephant is captured, it is trained for seven months and then sold to an owner who hires the services of a *mahout*. A *mahout* may change elephants several times.

MORANE

Among the Masai tribes, the Moranes are the males who have been initiated. Initiation takes place every seven years, during a secret celebration. Moranes of all ages, from sixteen to twenty-eight, gather for two days and two nights for the initiation. One phase of the initiation involves shaving the head and eyebrows. Once

initiated, a Morane is allowed to marry. The transition from the status of a Morane to that of a married man has no sexual implications. For the Masai, this feast is not a joyful occasion, for it marks the end of one's life as a Morane.

ASIATIC WILD ASS

A wild donkey that has become extremely rare. This wild ass has been so hunted, by Jeep and helicopter, that there are only a few groups of them scattered about. Formerly, it was plentiful in Iran and the south of Russia. A herd is being developed on an Israeli preserve.

ORYX

An African and Asian antelope represented by several species. The Arabian oryx is the smallest and rarest. It was once found throughout Arabia, in the Sinai desert and in Mesopotamia. When the species was about to become extinct in the wild, a breeding herd was formed on a preserve in Arizona from several survivors gathered from zoos. The number in captivity is still not sufficiently large to warrant releasing any of them in the wild.

PANADUS

A tropical plant having a cactuslike trunk and tufts of leaves. The pandanus is used in Polynesia to roof houses. It is said to keep out the rain and to moderate the temperature within the houses, but it is a relatively expensive building material. In the Seychelles, and especially on Cousin Island, these trees are covered with terns' nests.

PRESERVE

A preserve is a parcel of undeveloped land in which the plants and animals are placed under protection. The extent of their effectiveness varies with the country in which it is located and the governmental regulations.

TAPIR

The tapir is a mammal found in Central and South America and Asia. It belongs to the same order as horses. There is only one species in Asia: the Indian tapir, which has a bi-colored coat. In South America, tapirs are smaller, and newborn tapirs have striped coats. Tapirs are semi-aquatic animals, but some of them live in the mountains. Their natural enemies are the tiger and the jaguar. They are timid, grass-eating animals and they feed at night. But we have seen some along the Amazon, in broad daylight, grazing in a marsh.

VICUÑA

The vicuña, a cousin of the lama and the guanaco, lives high on the plateaux of the Andes. It was considered by the Incas to be "the queen of animals." At that time, vicuñas were plentiful, but so many of them were killed for their wool that there are now no more than a few hundred specimens surviving. The government of Peru, advised by the W.W.F., has taken steps to protect the vicuña. But only the lack of demand for vicuña coats can ensure the preservation of this species on a permanent basis.

VIVERRIN

A family of carnivorous mammals including the civet, genet, mongoose, and others. The bodies are slender with long tails and short legs. They are animals that feed at night, primarily on small animals and vegetable matter.

Bibliography

Gee, E.P. *The Wildlife of India.* New York: E.P. Dutton & Co., Inc., 1972.

Grzimek, Bernard. *Rhinoceros Belong to Everybody.* London: William Collins Sons & Co., Ltd., 1964.

Henvelmans, Bernard. *Sur la Piste des Betes Ignorees.* Paris: Librairie Plon S.A., 1955.

International Union for Conservation of Nature. *Red Data Book.* Vol. 1: Mammalia; Vol. 2: Mammalia; Vol. 3: Aves; Vol. 4: Amphibiant et Reptilia. Laussanne, Switzerland: Arts Graphiques Heliographia S.A., 1972.

La Faune: Vie et Moeurs des Animaux Sauvages. Paris: Grande Bateliere S.A., no date.

Lorenz, Konrad. *Il Parlait avec les Mammiferes, les Oiseaux et les Poissons.* Paris: Flammarion et Cie, 1968.

Marler, Peter R. et al. *The Marvels of Animal Behavior.* Washington, D.C.: National Geographic Society, 1972.

Pfeffer, Pierre and Guy Dhuit. *Zoo Sans Frontieres.* Paris: Librairie Hatiere S.A., 1970.

Schulthesa, Emile. *Afrique, de la Mediterranee a l'Equateur.* Zurich: Robert Delpire, 1958.

Simon and Gerondet. *Survivants.* Lausanne: Edita S.A., no date.

Spinage, C.A. *Animaux Sauvages d'Afrique.* Paris: Editions Stock, 1962.

Acknowledgements and credits

The author and his team would like to express their gratitude to all who contributed to their numerous expeditions throughout the world. Special thanks are due to the following:

His Royal Highness, Prince Bernhard of the Netherlands: Their Excellencies Madam Indira Gandhi, President Jomo Kenyatta, and James Macnam, Minister to Seychelles.

The embassies of Ecuador, Malaysia, Kenya, Tanzania, India, South Africa, Sri Lanka, and Singapore.

O.R.S.T.O.M. personnel in French Guiana.

The airlines that have not only facilitated traveling but have also signed a protocol for the protection of nature: U.T.A., Air France, Air India, Malaisia A.S., and Avianca.

The author would also like personally to thank the various media: television (O.R.F.T. Swiss Television, Belgian Television, Canadian Television); radio (O.R.T.F., Europe, Luxembourg, Monte Carlo); the press (*Tele 7 Jours, Paris-Match, le Figaro, France-Soir, le Parisien Libere, l'Aurore, l'Humanite, l'Alsace, le Sud-Ouest, Ouest-France, Nice-Matin, Tintin, Betes et Nature, Loisirs et Nature,* and *Life Magazine*).

We owe special thanks to *Vogue* and *Harpers Bazaar* for having explained so clearly to their readers the problems of survival of the spotted cats, and for declaring that they would accept no advertising for these furs. One can only recognize the financial sacrifice involved, and thank the publishers of these magazines for their dedication to nature.

All photographs in this book are the property of Christian and Nadine Zuber, with the exception of several taken by Michel Laubreaux, Pierre Loustau, and Bruno Barbey. We wish to thank Professor Yves Coppens for having allowed us to reproduce some material on elephants as well as his line drawings on the origins of elephants.

Maps and drawings: Dieter Wagner
Layout: Yves Raynaud and Christian Zuber.
Production: Galápagos-Films.

Dépôt légal 2e trimestre 1974 - Flammarion, éditeur, N° 9935 - N° d'imp. : 6607.
Imprimerie Déchaux, 93 Aulnay-sous-Bois - Printed in France.